JAZZ PIANO SOLOS     VOLUME 23

# jazz for lovers

Arranged by Brent Edstrom

T0071665

## contents

ISBN 978-1-4584-2101-2

HAL•LEONARD®
CORPORATION

7777 W. BLUEMOUND RD. P.O. BOX 13819 MILWAUKEE, WI 53213

Visit Hal Leonard Online at
www.halleonard.com

# BEYOND THE SEA

Lyrics by JACK LAWRENCE
Music by CHARLES TRENET and ALBERT LASRY
Original French Lyric to "La Mer" by CHARLES TRENET

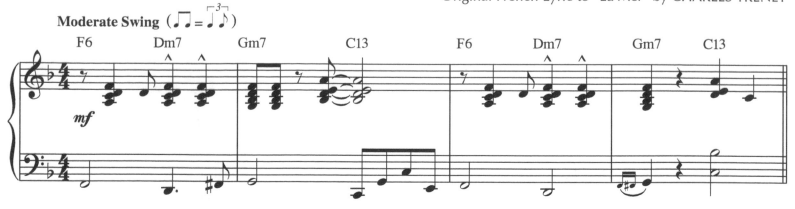

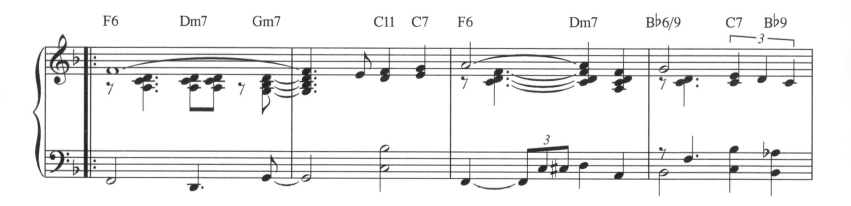

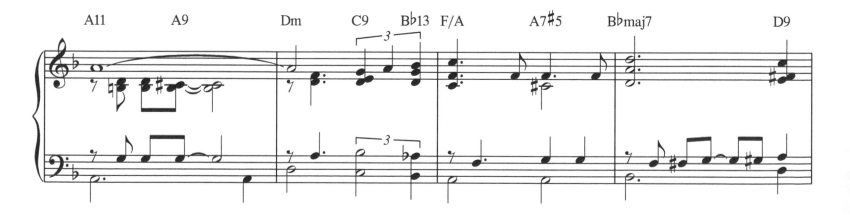

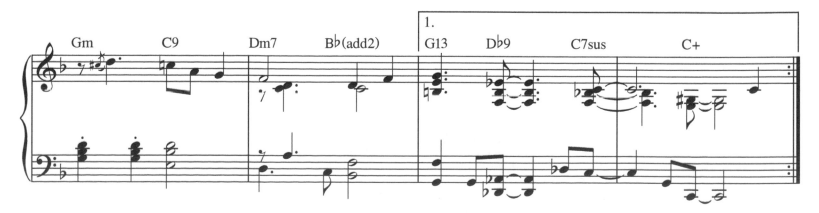

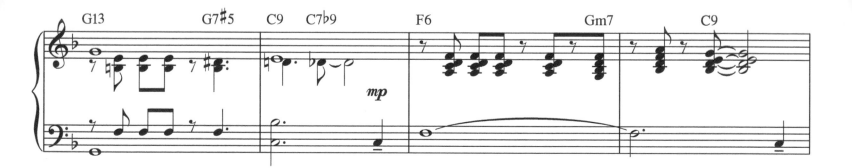

# BILL
## from SHOW BOAT

Music by JEROME KERN
Words by P.G. WODEHOUSE
and OSCAR HAMMERSTEIN II

Slowly, with rubato

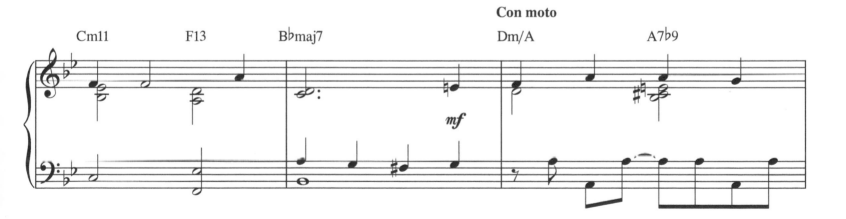

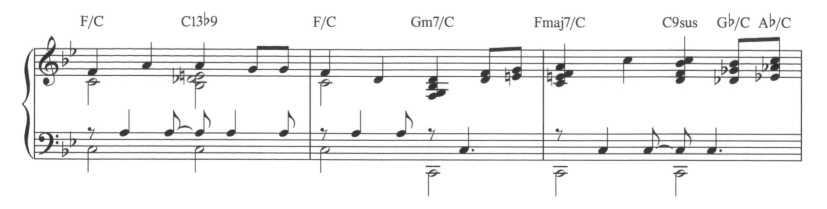

**Medium Swing**

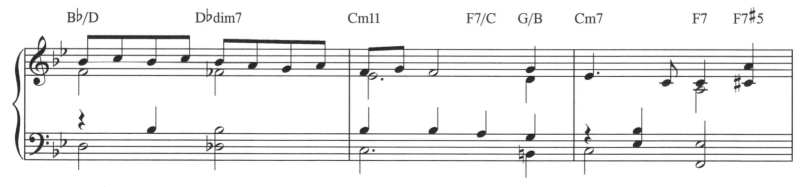

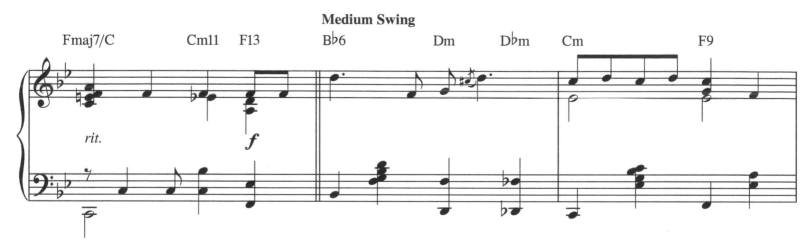

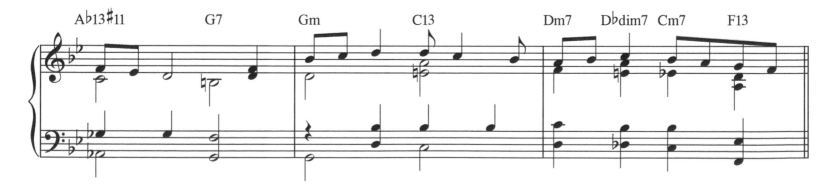

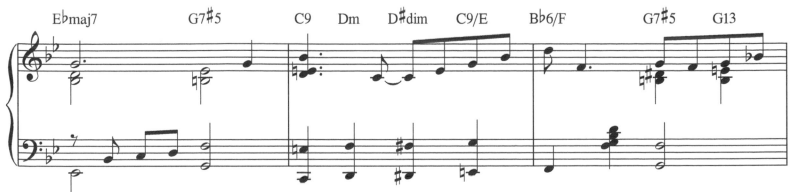

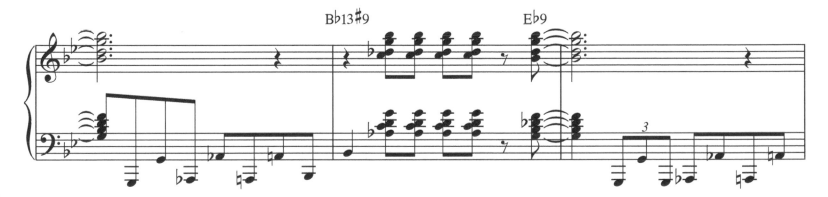

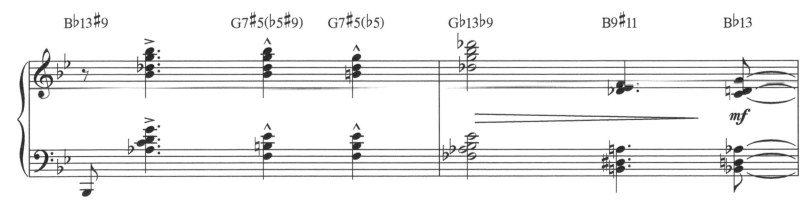

# BUT BEAUTIFUL

Words by JOHNNY BURKE<br>Music by JIMMY VAN HEUSEN

**Ballad, with rubato**

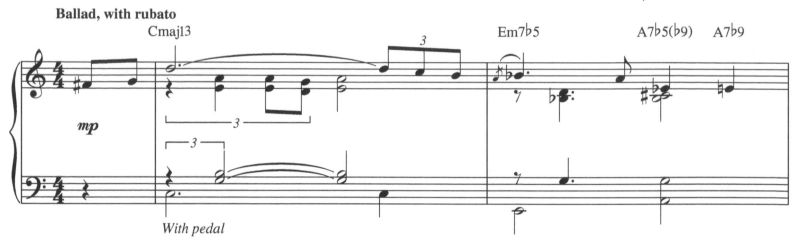

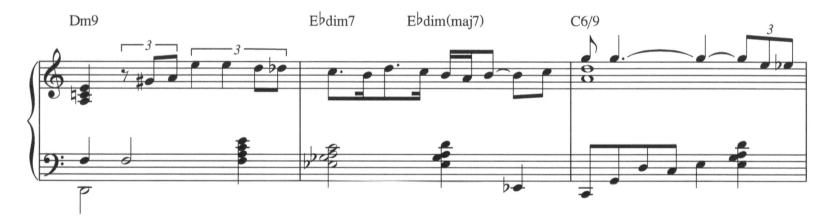

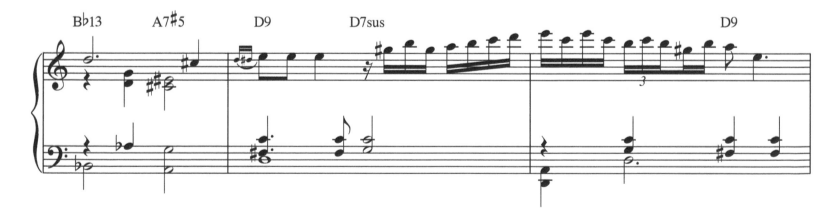

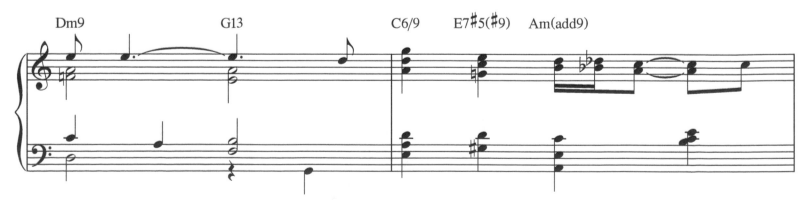

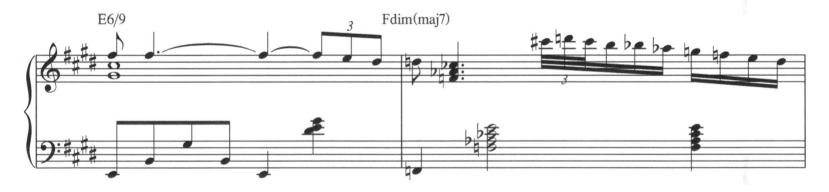

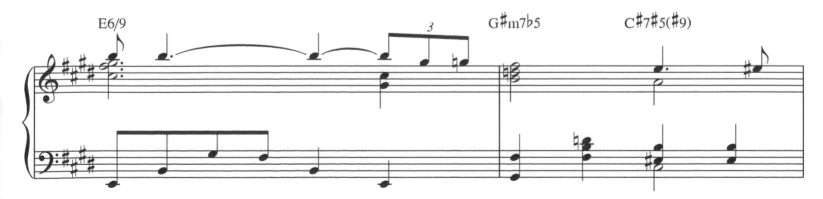

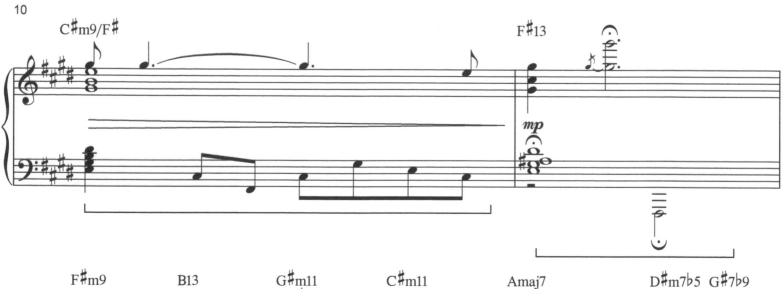

# FOR ALL WE KNOW

Words by SAM M. LEWIS
Music by J. FRED COOTS

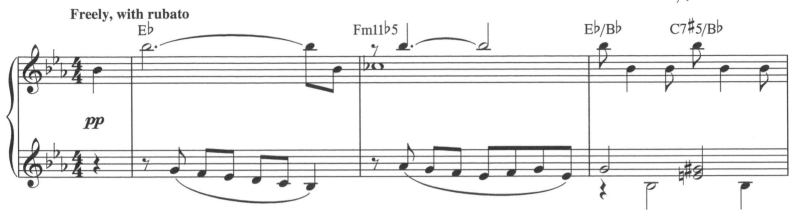

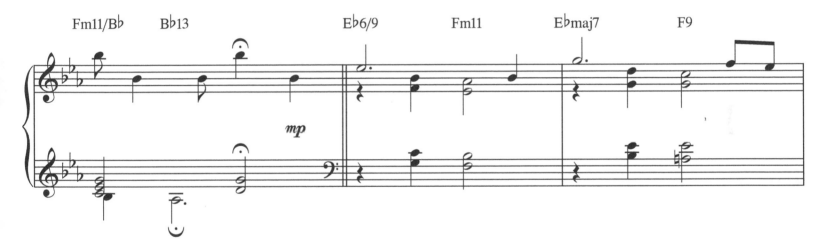

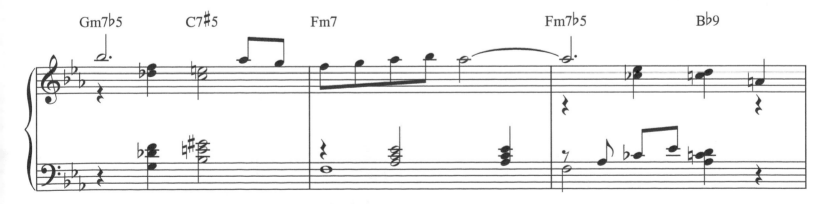

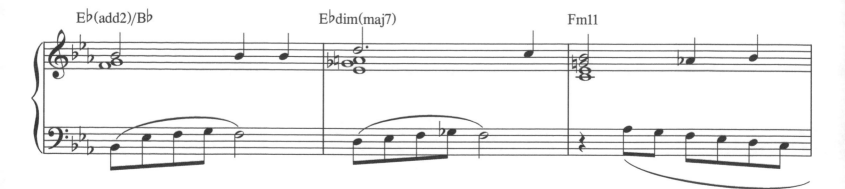

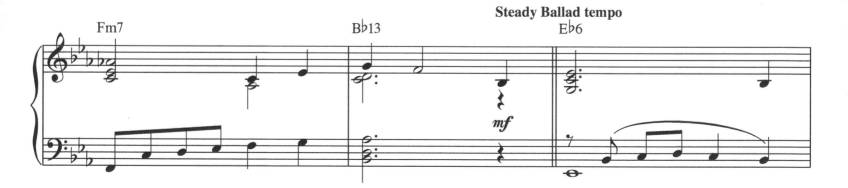

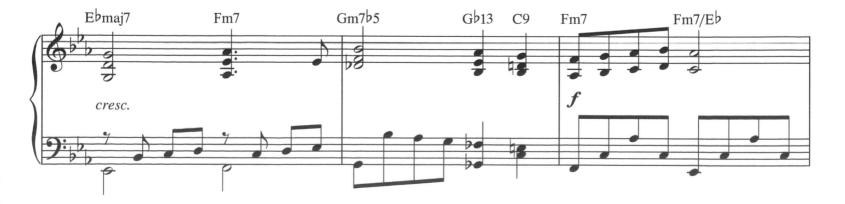

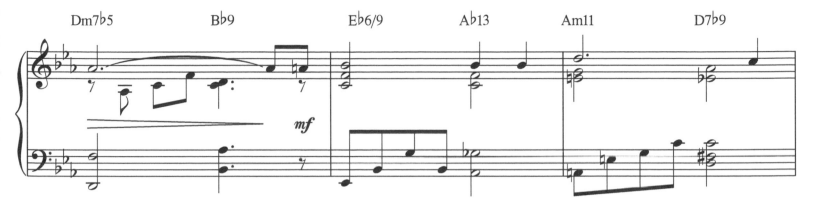

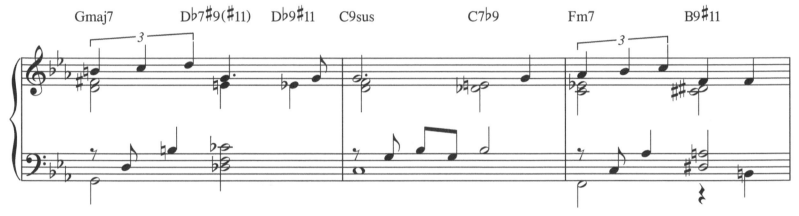

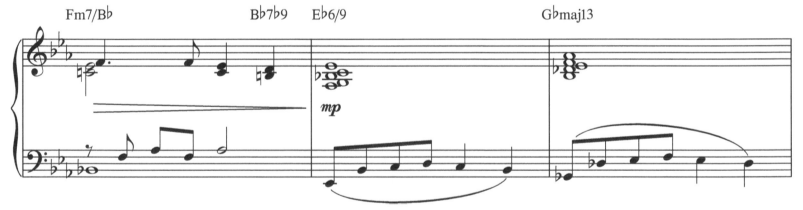

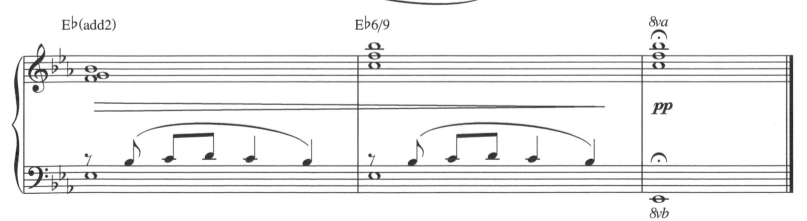

# DARN THAT DREAM

Lyric by EDDIE DE LANGE
Music by JIMMY VAN HEUSEN

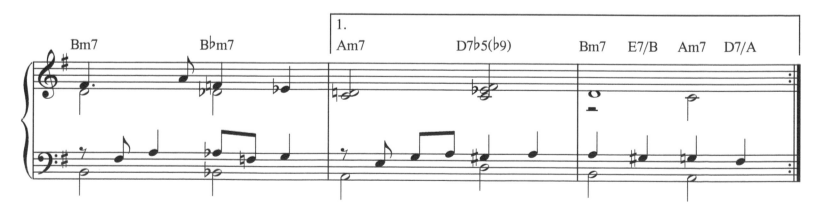

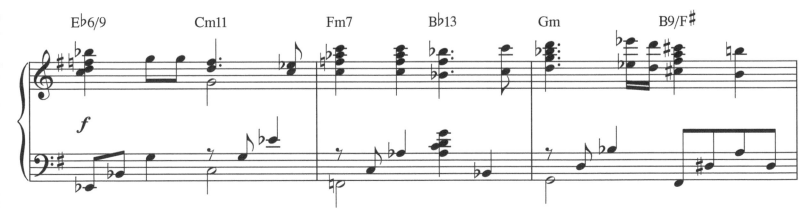

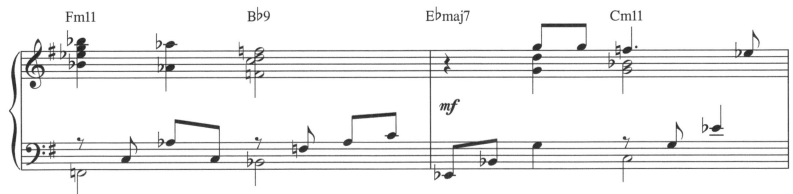

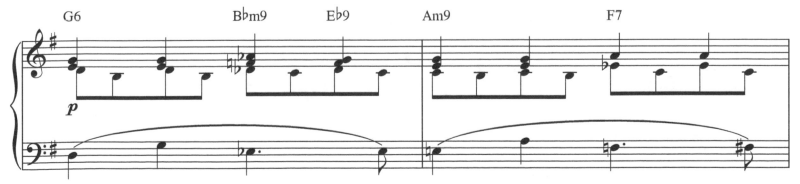

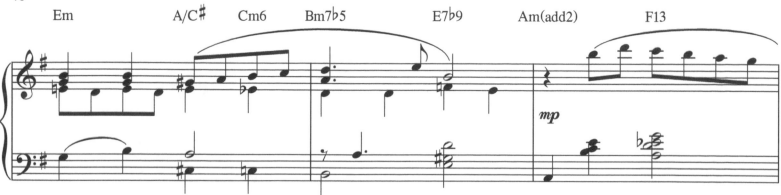

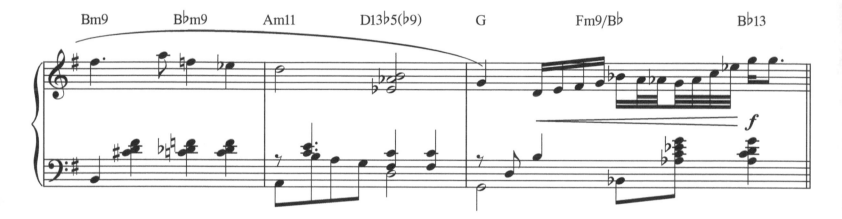

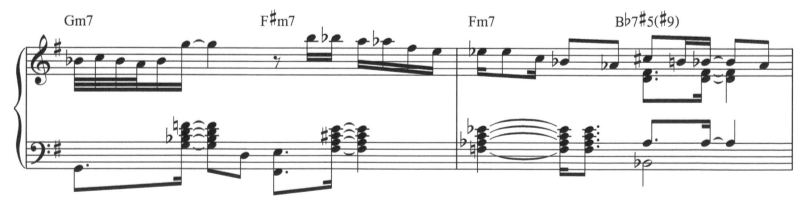

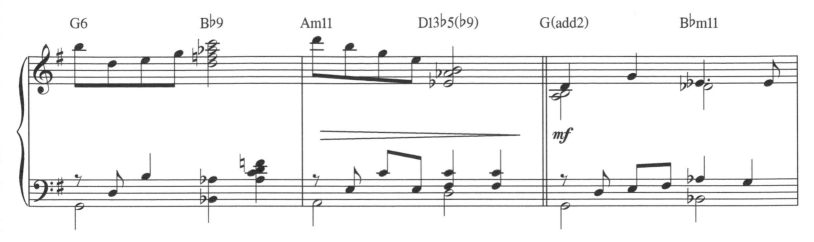

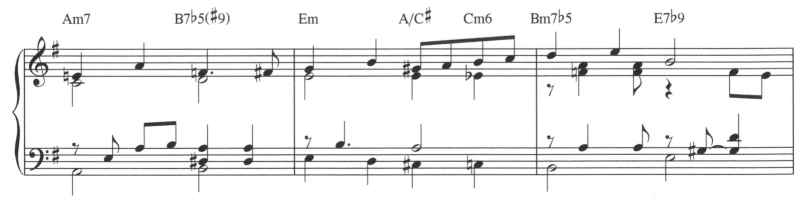

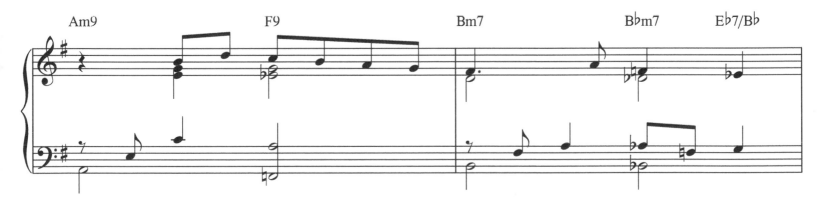

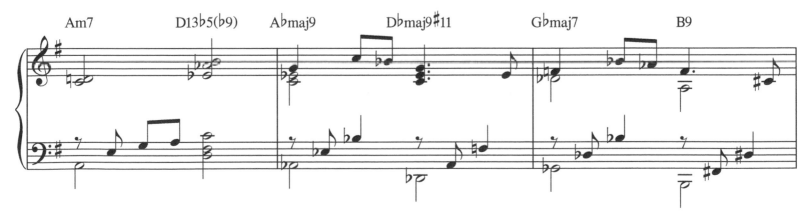

# HERE'S THAT RAINY DAY

Words by JOHNNY BURKE
Music by JIMMY VAN HEUSEN

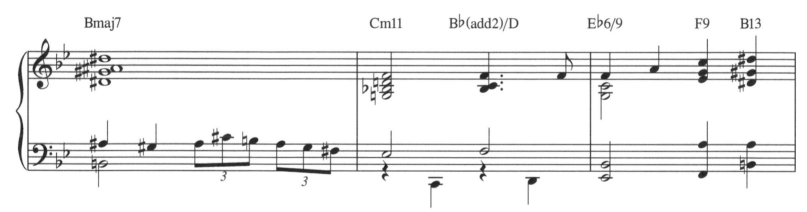

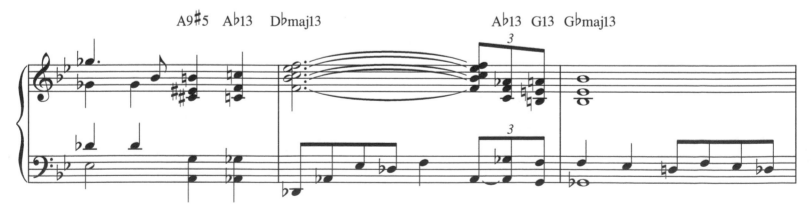

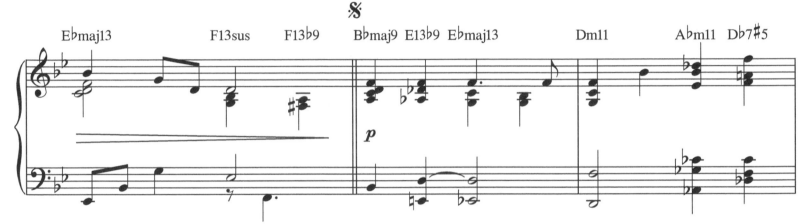

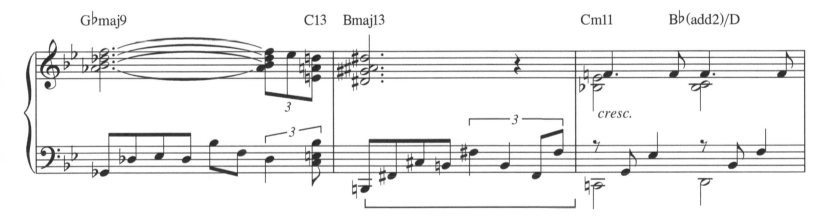

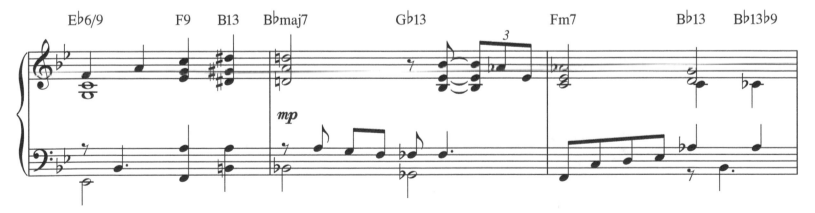

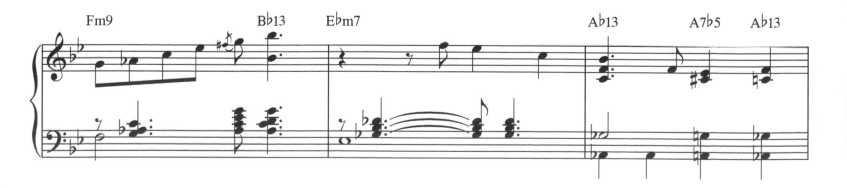

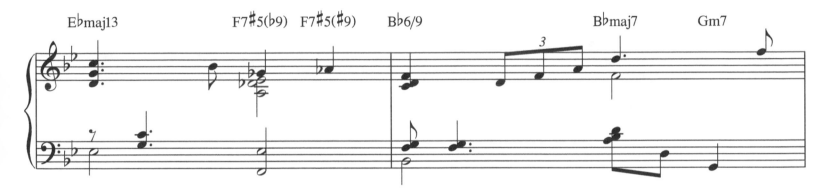

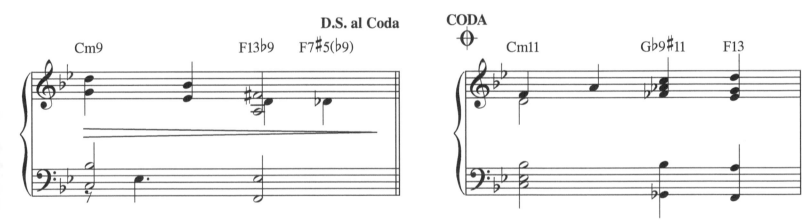

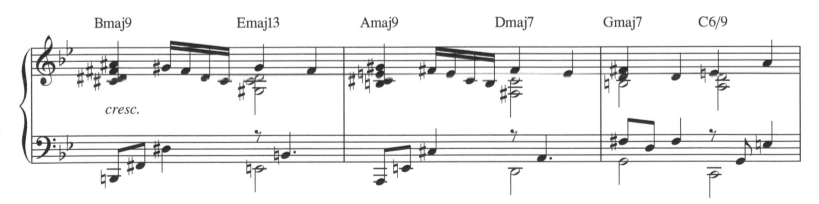

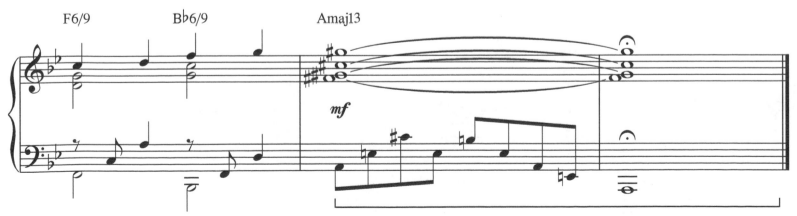

# I CAN'T BELIEVE THAT YOU'RE IN LOVE WITH ME

Words and Music by JIMMY McHUGH
and CLARENCE GASKILL

**Relaxed Swing**

*Left hand like a rhythm guitar*    *sim.*

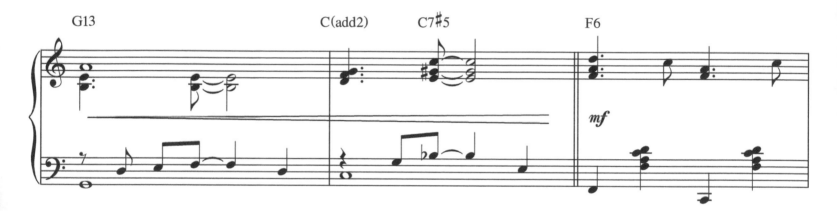

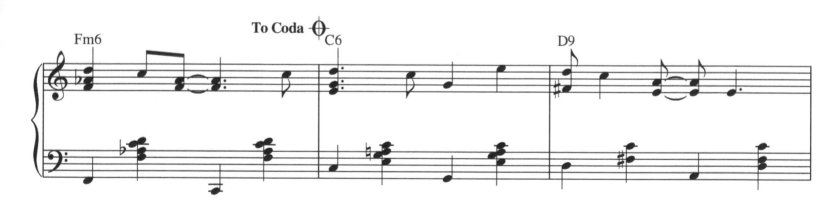

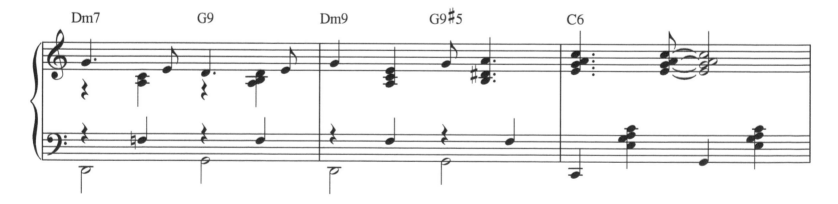

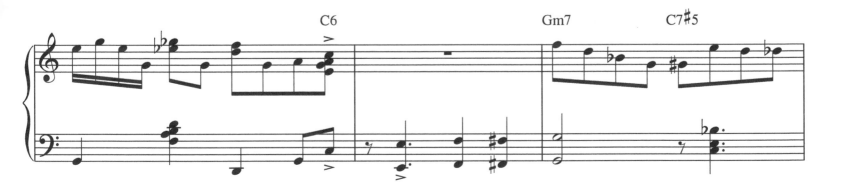

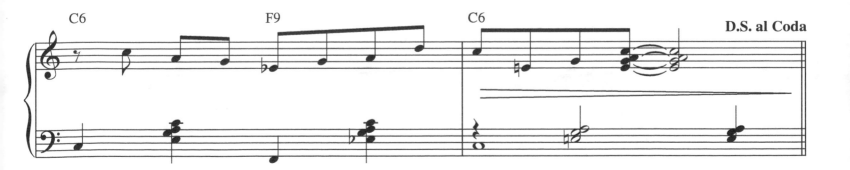

26

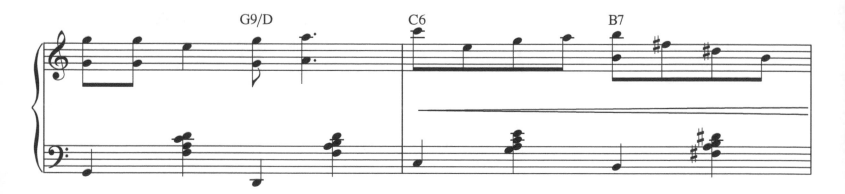

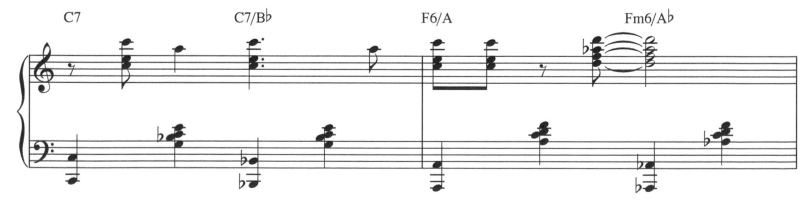

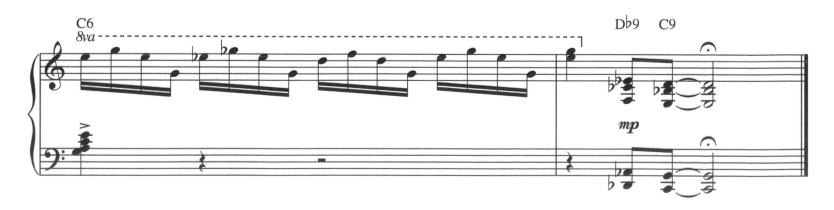

# I DIDN'T KNOW WHAT TIME IT WAS

from TOO MANY GIRLS

Words by LORENZ HART
Music by RICHARD RODGERS

**Slowly, with rubato**

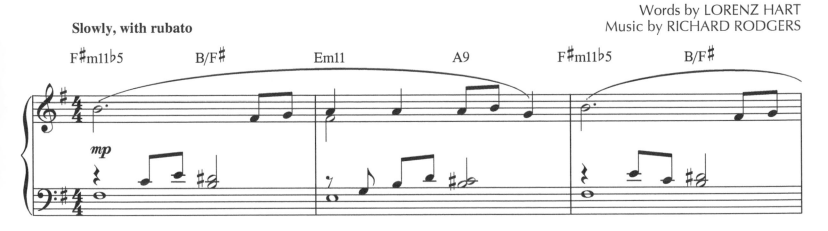

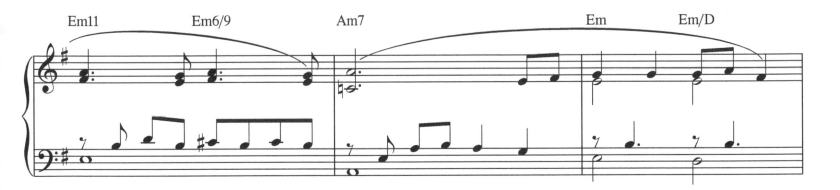

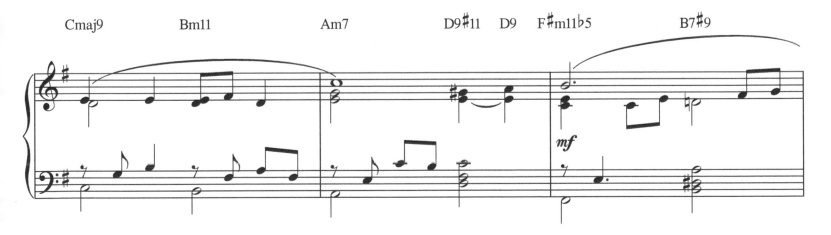

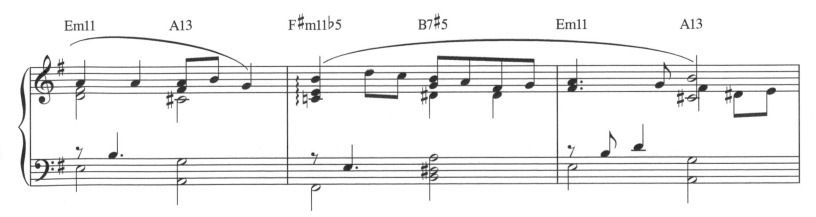

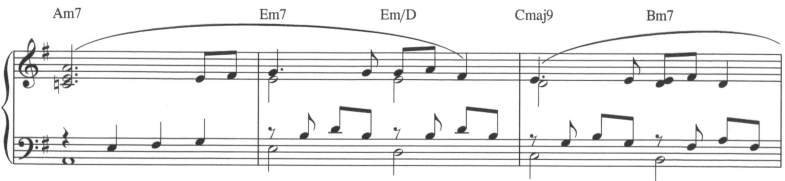

**Medium Swing**

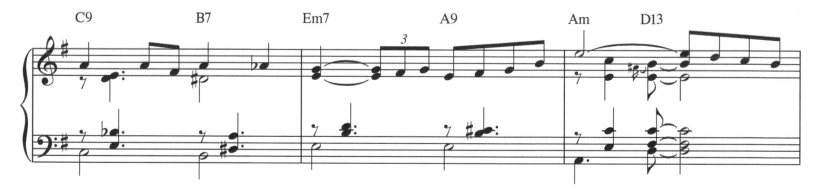

**Ballad tempo, with motion**

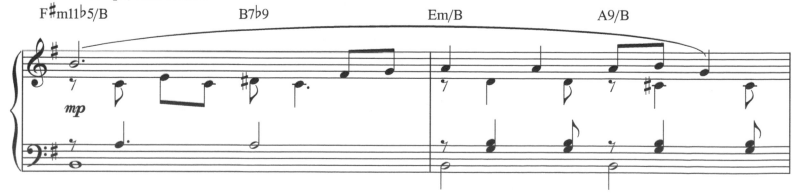

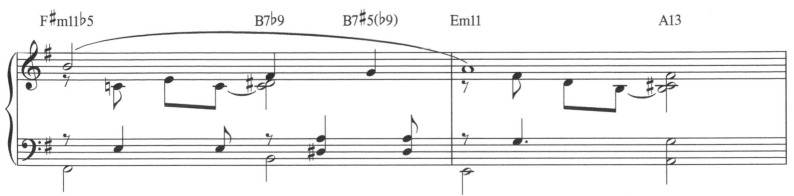

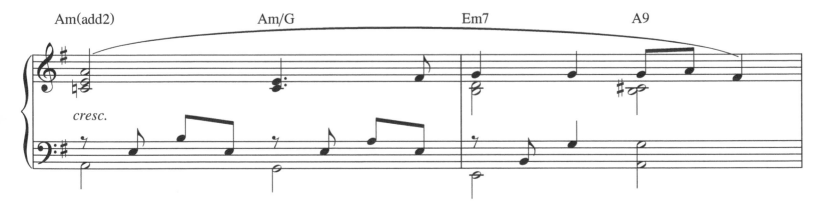

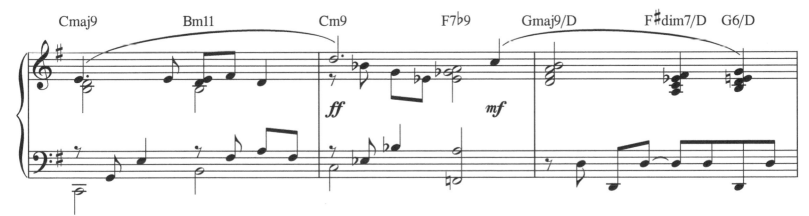

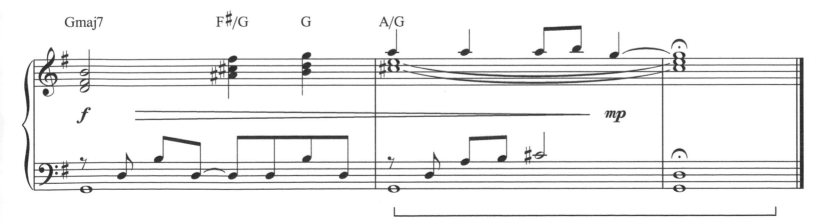

# I SHOULD CARE

Words and Music by SAMMY CAHN,
PAUL WESTON and AXEL STORDAHL

**Ballad, with rubato**

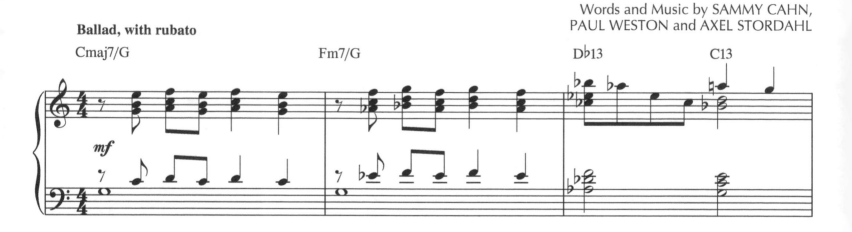

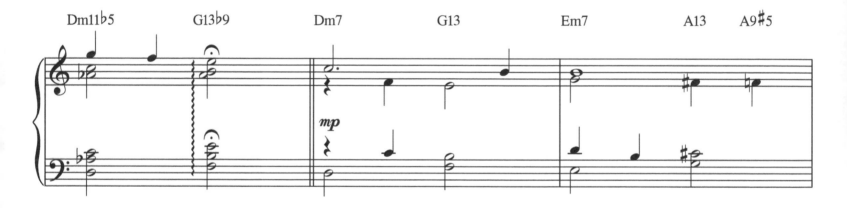

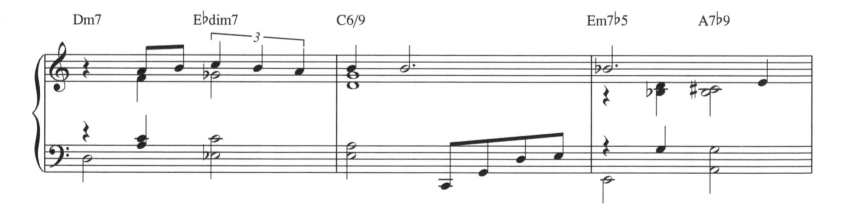

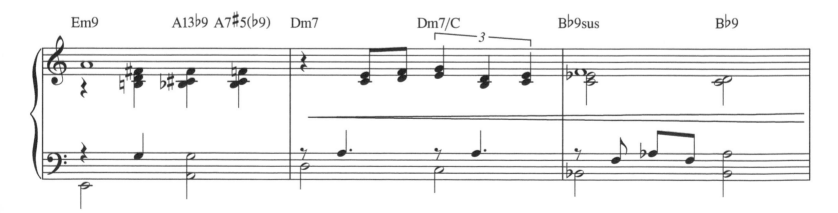

**Flowing, with a steady beat**

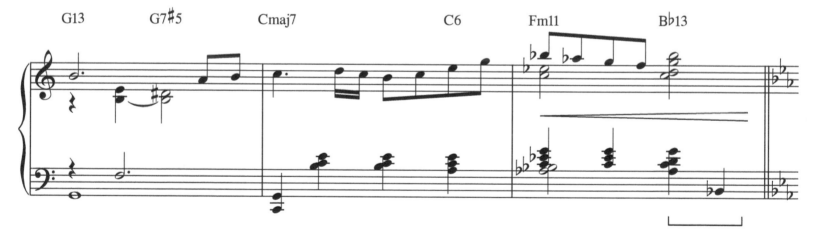

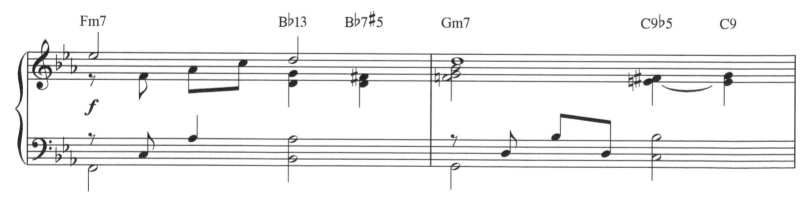

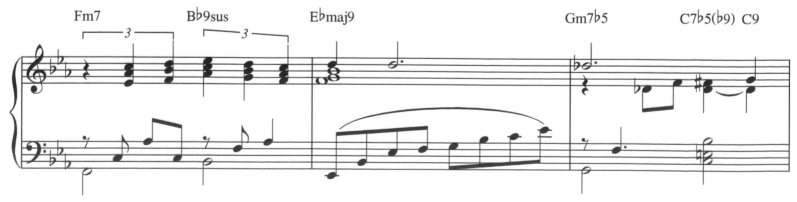

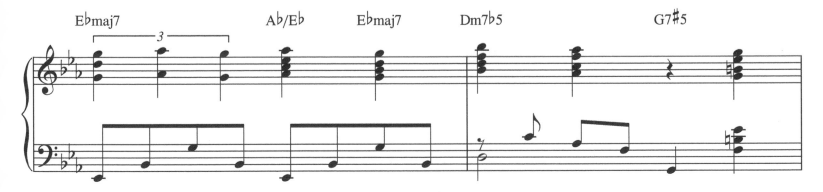

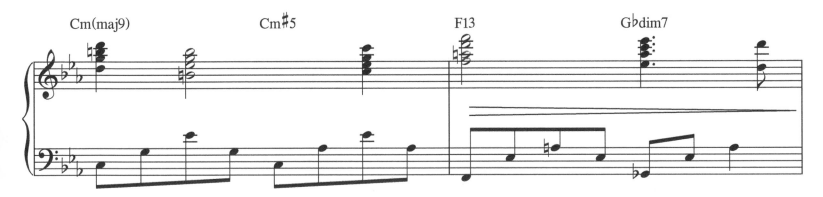

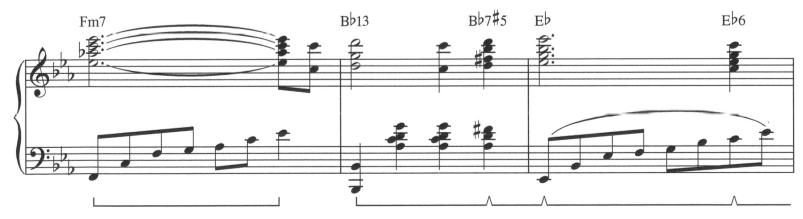

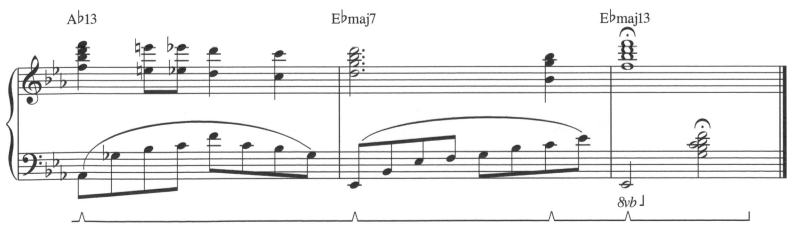

# I THOUGHT ABOUT YOU

Words by JOHNNY MERCER
Music by JIMMY VAN HEUSEN

**Medium Swing**

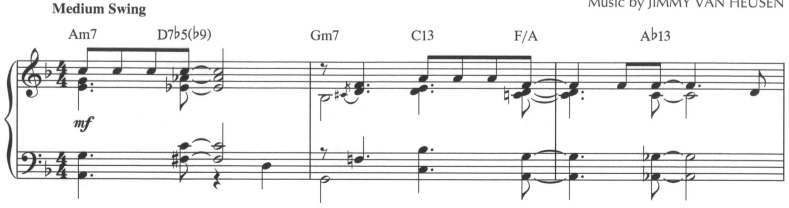

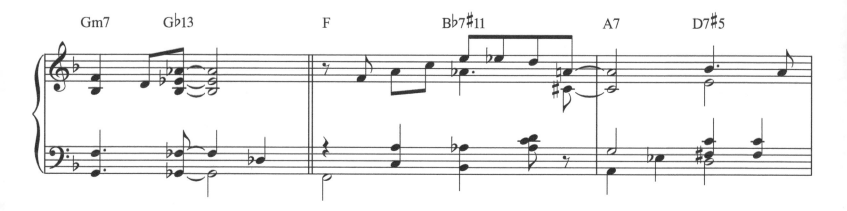

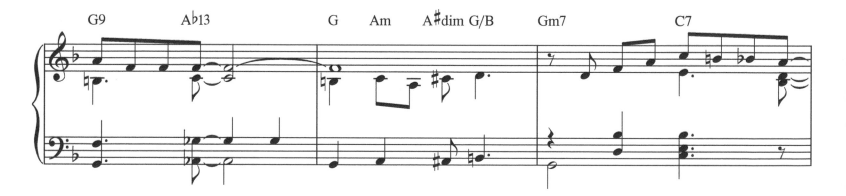

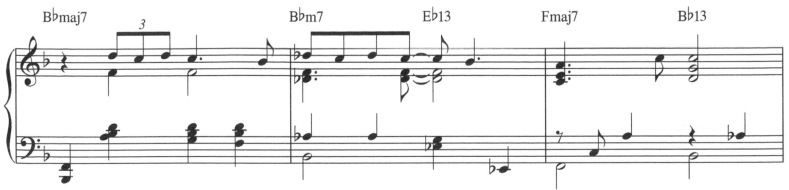

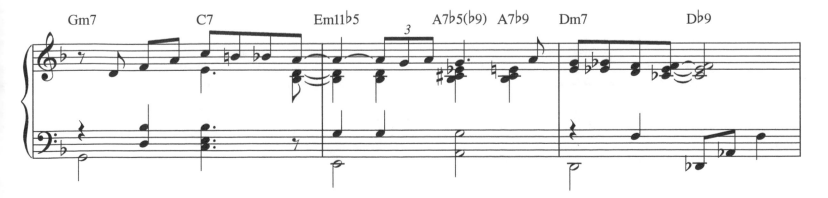

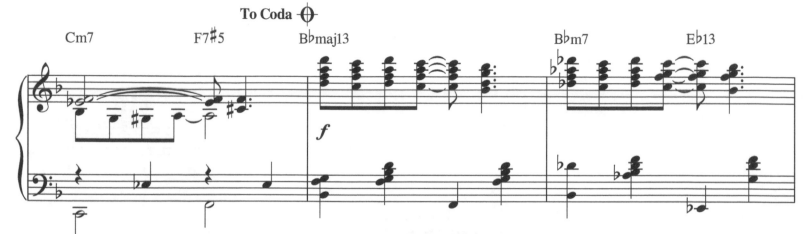

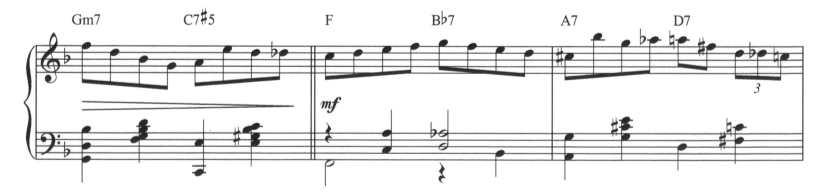

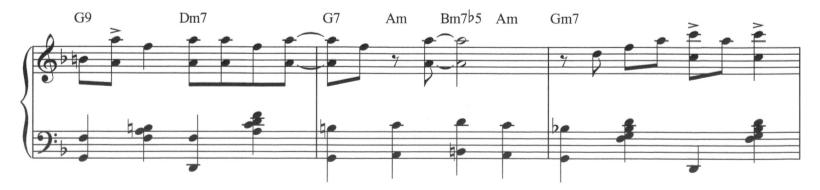

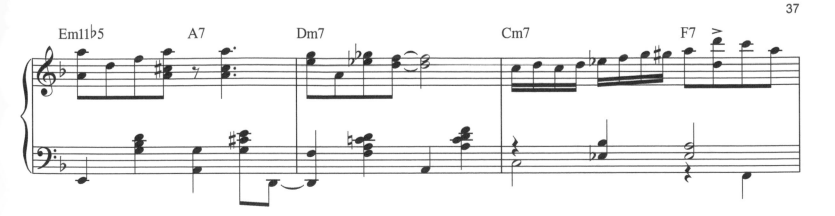

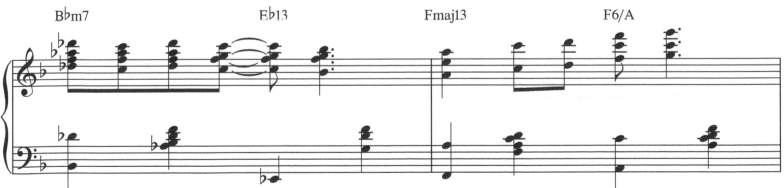

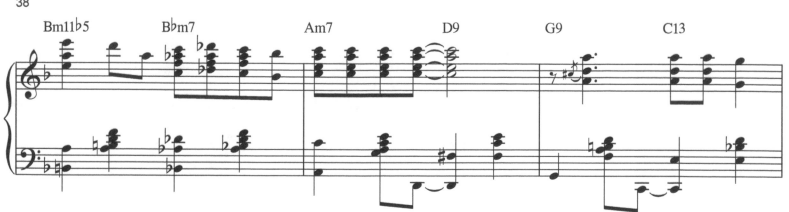

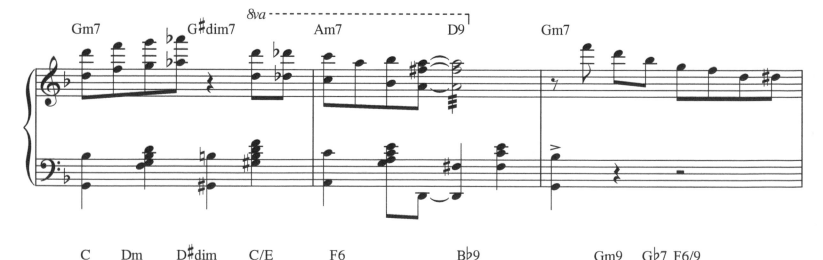

# IF I SHOULD LOSE YOU

from the Paramount Picture ROSE OF THE RANCHO

Words and Music by LEO ROBIN
and RALPH RAINGER

Medium Swing

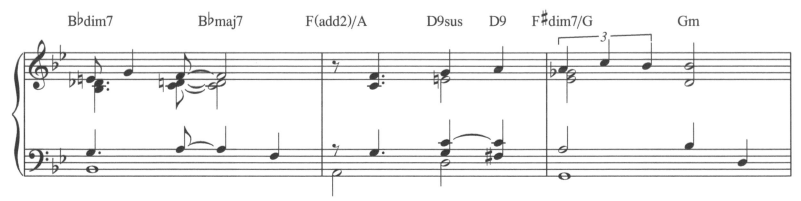

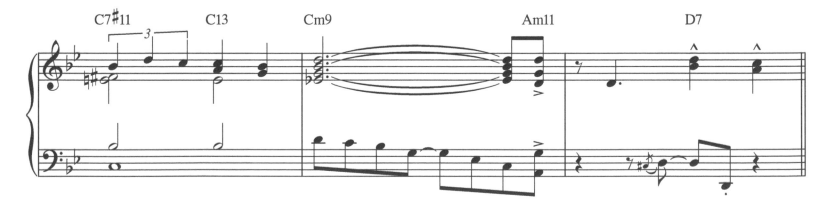

To Coda ⊕

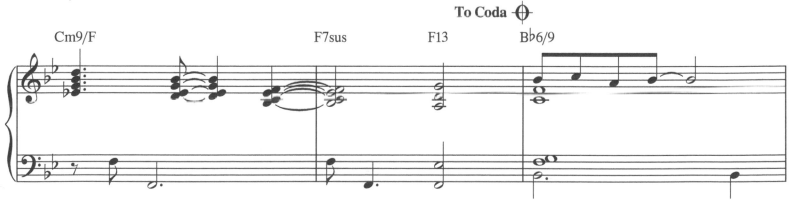

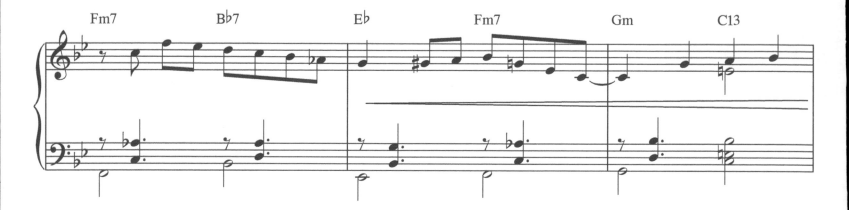

**CODA**

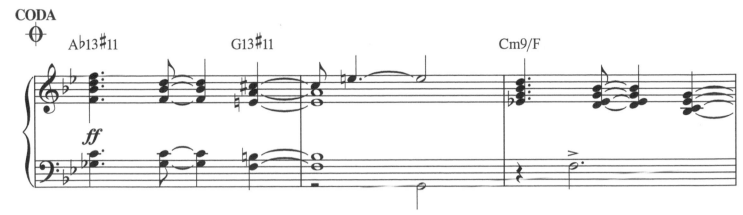

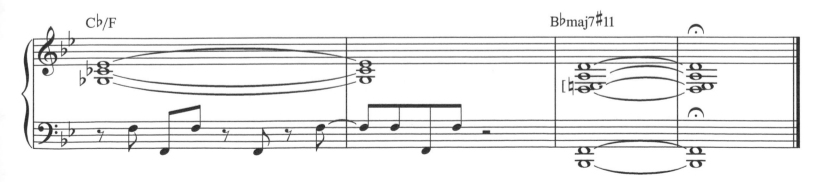

# IMAGINATION

Words by JOHNNY BURKE
Music by JIMMY VAN HEUSEN

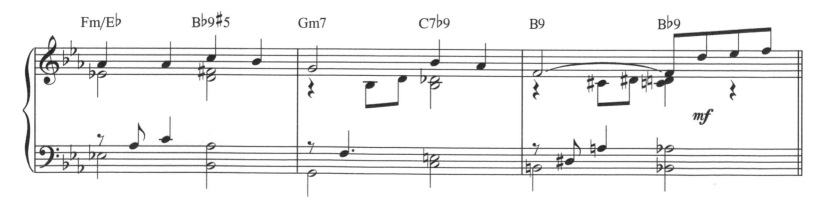

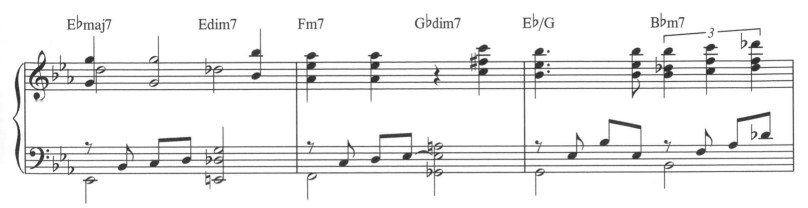

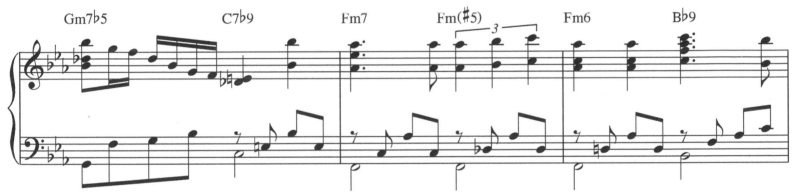

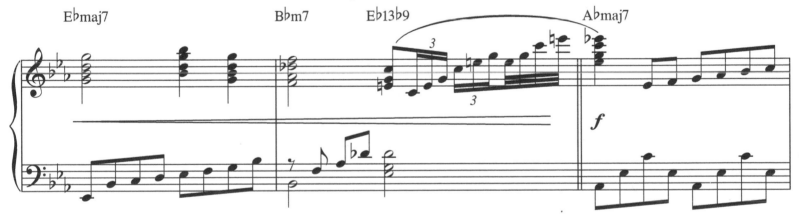

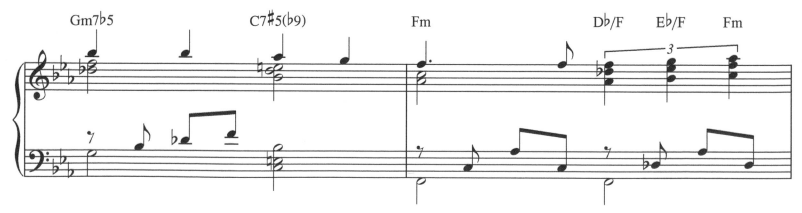

**Steady**

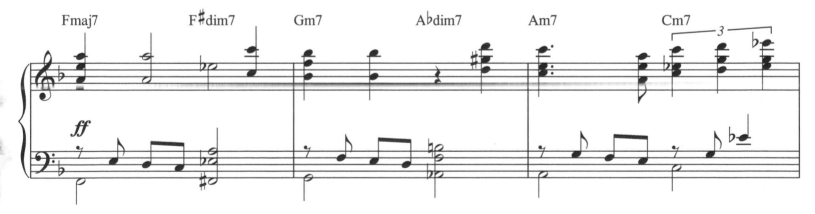

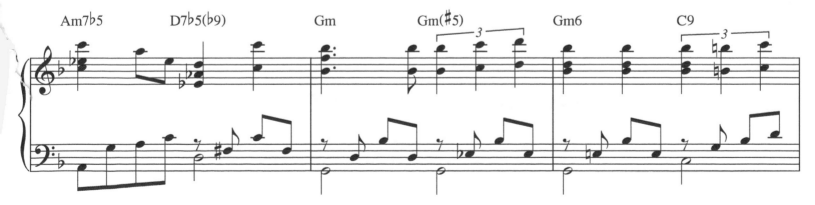

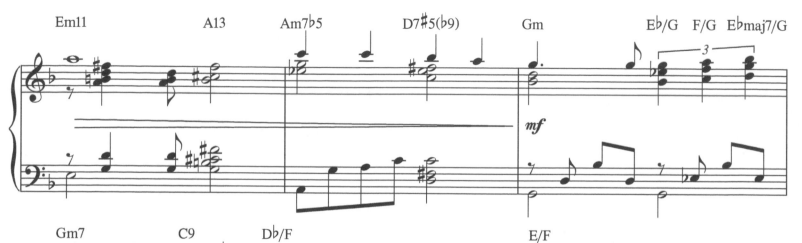

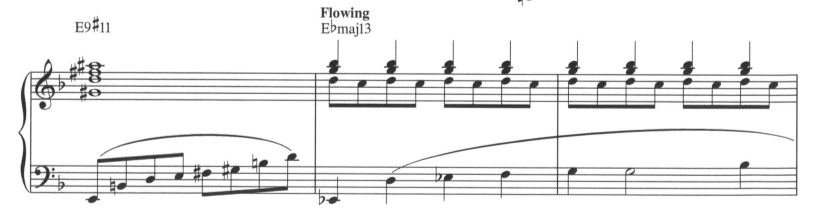

# A LOVELY WAY TO SPEND AN EVENING

Words by HAROLD ADAMSON
Music by JIMMY McHUGH

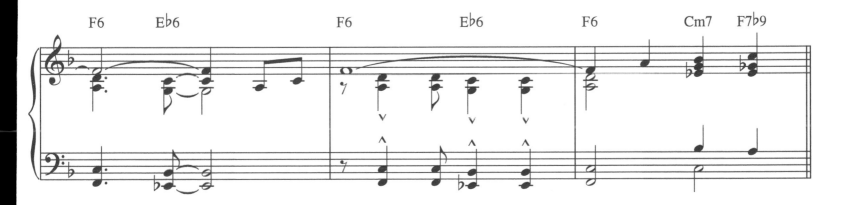

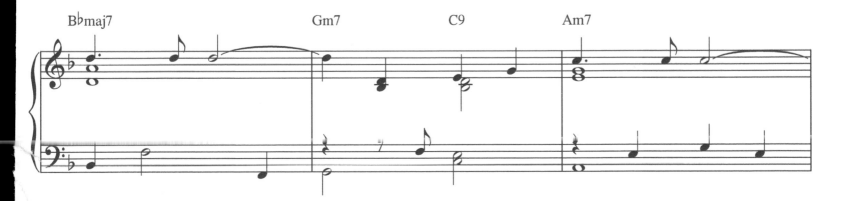

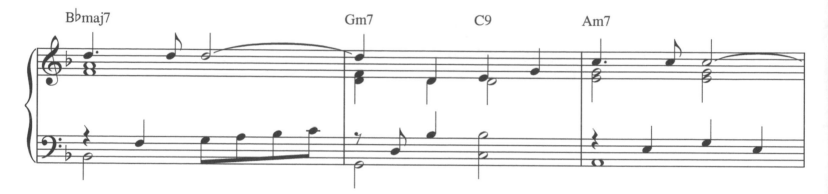

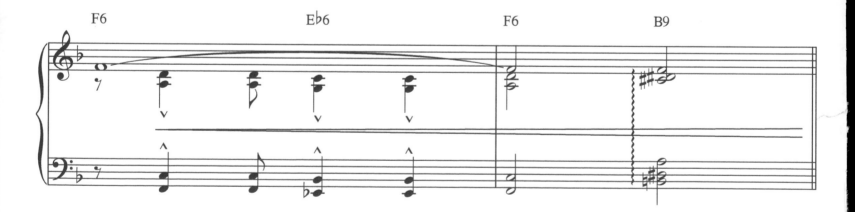

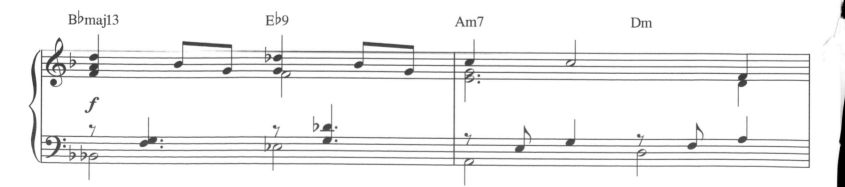

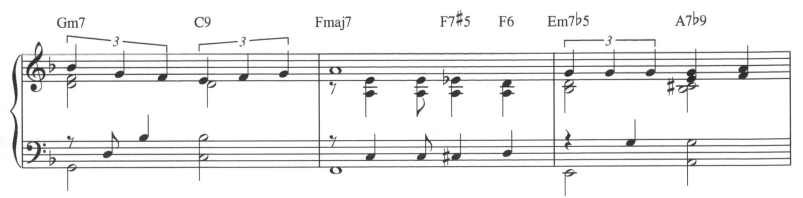

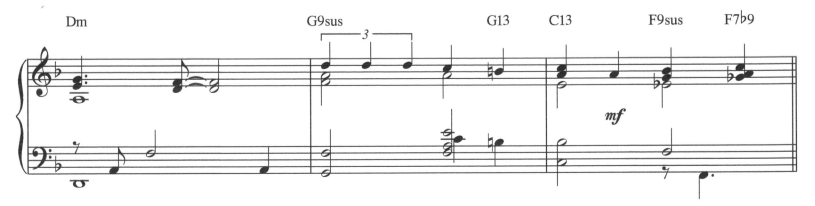

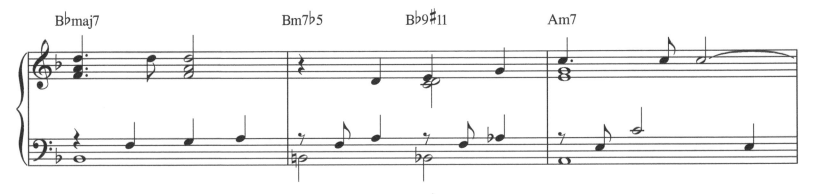

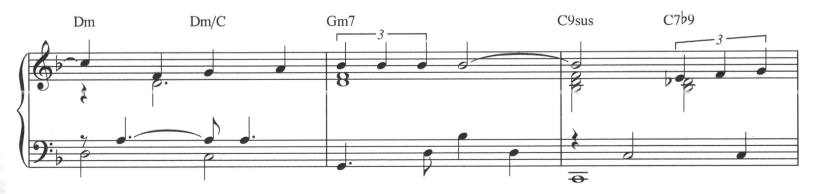

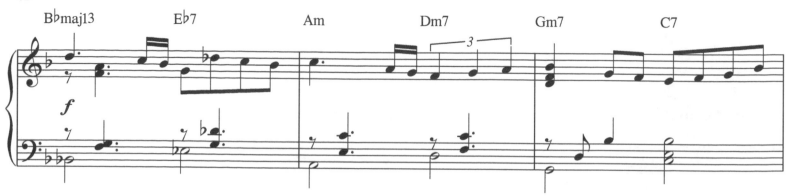

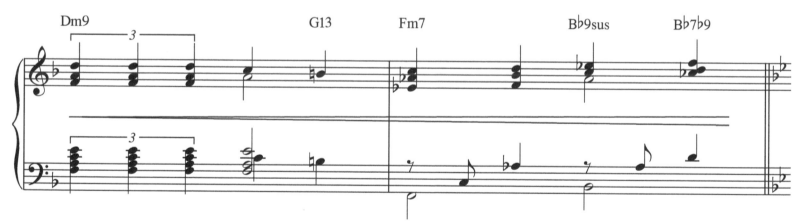

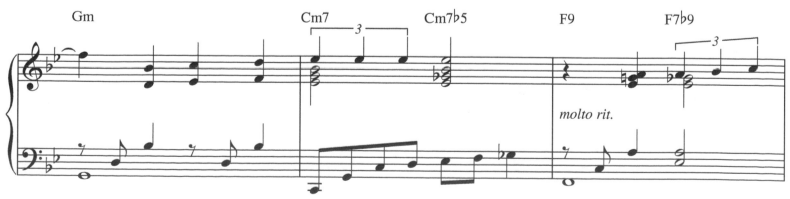

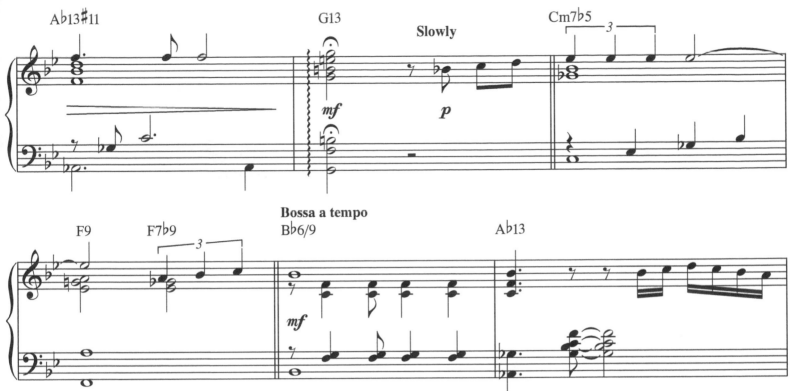

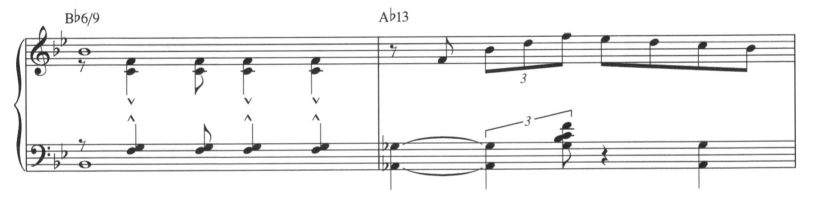

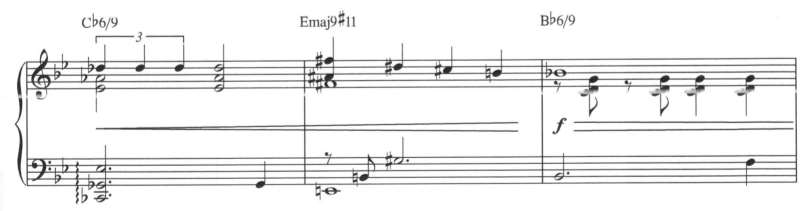

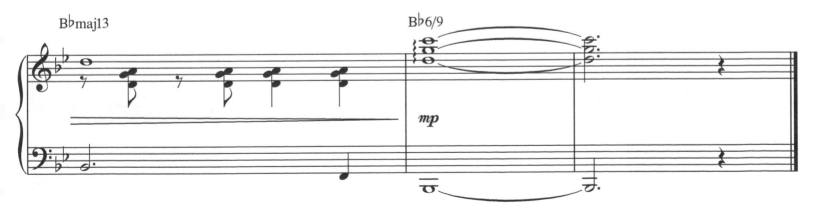

# MOONLIGHT IN VERMONT

Words by JOHN BLACKBURN
Music by KARL SUESSDORF

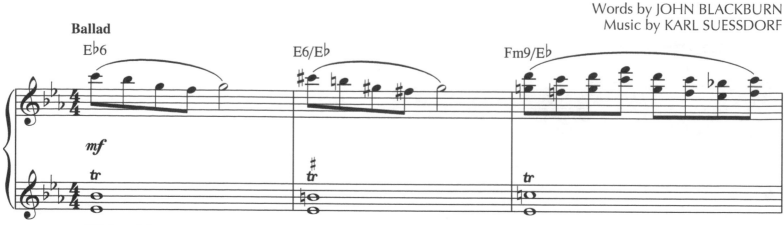

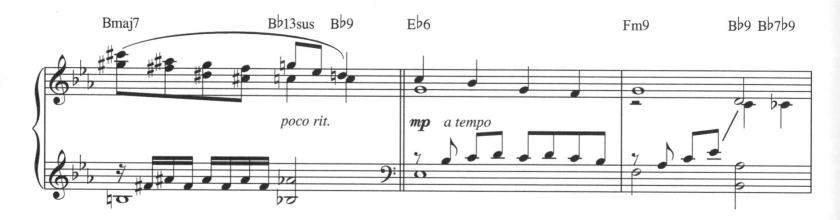

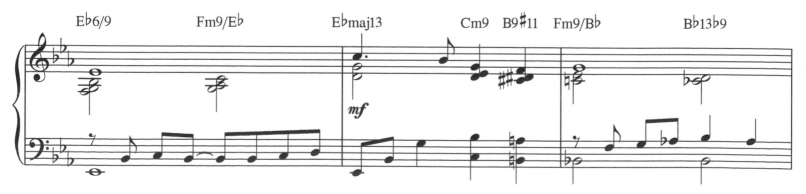

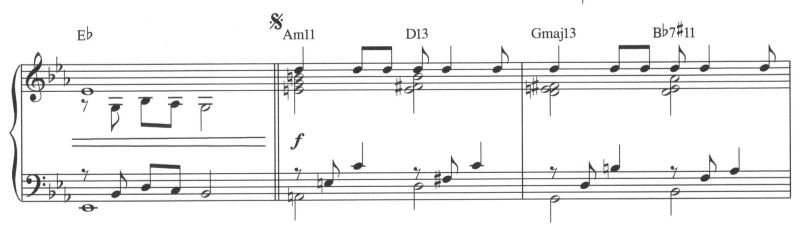

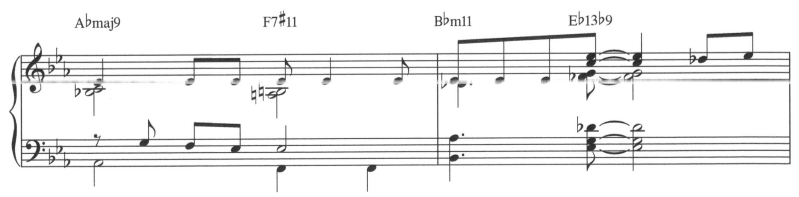

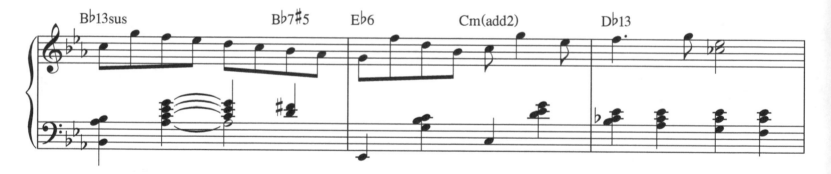

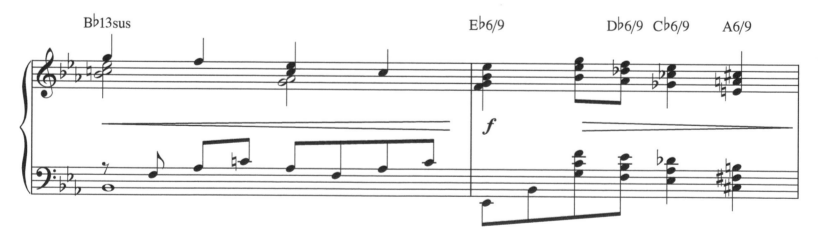

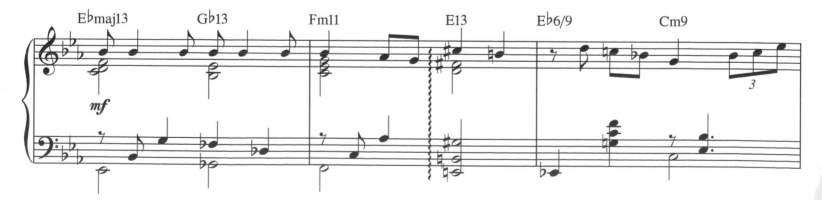

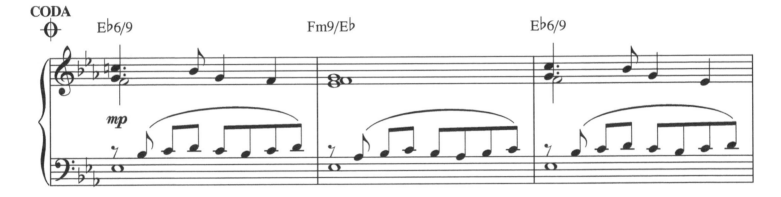

# MY ONE AND ONLY LOVE

Words by ROBERT MELLIN
Music by GUY WOOD

**Ballad, with rubato**

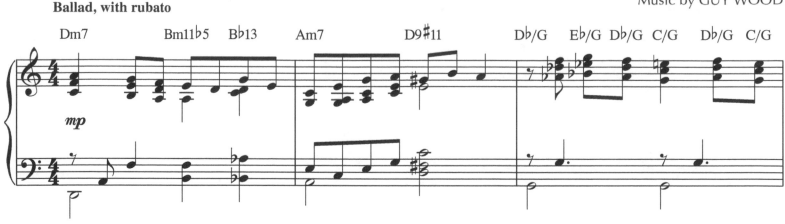

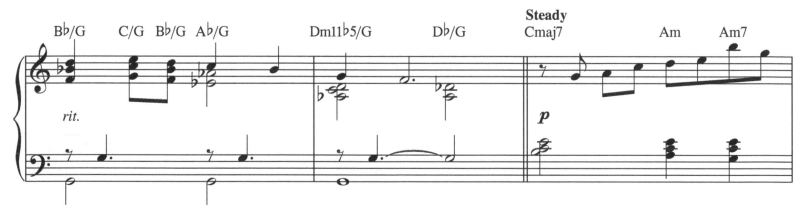

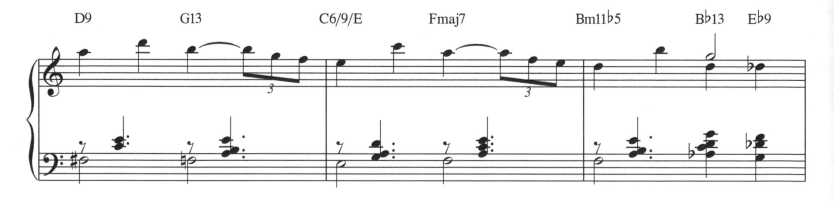

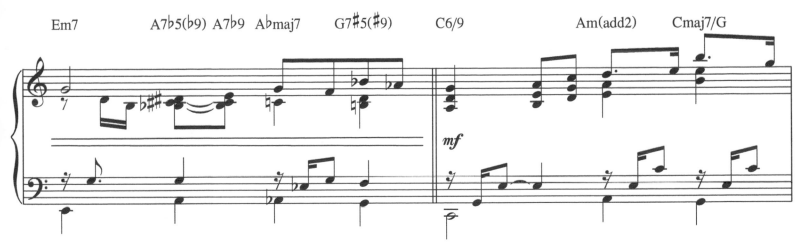

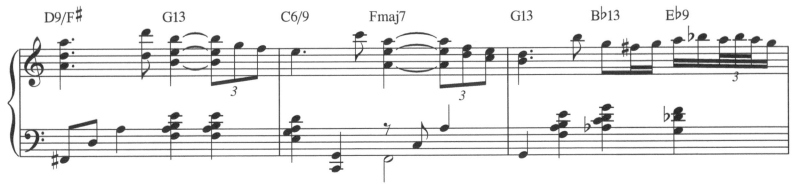

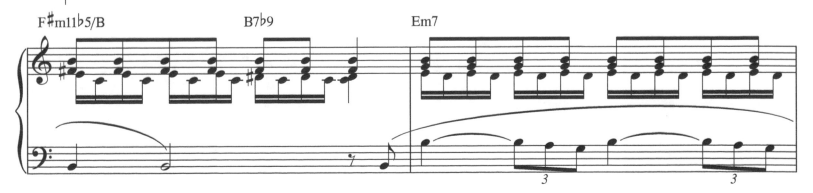

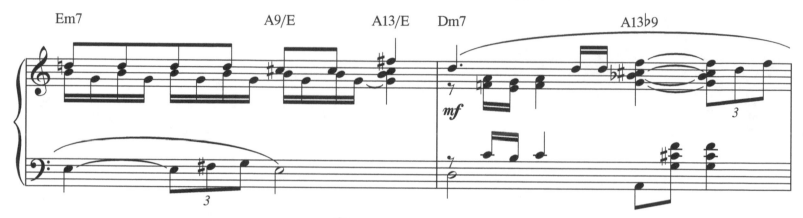

**D.S. al Coda**

**CODA**

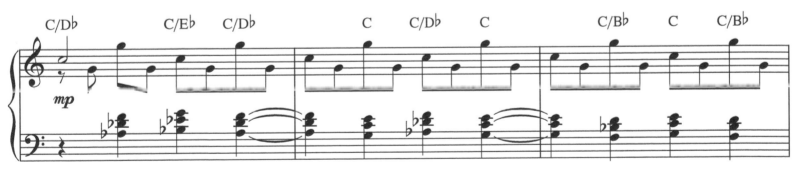

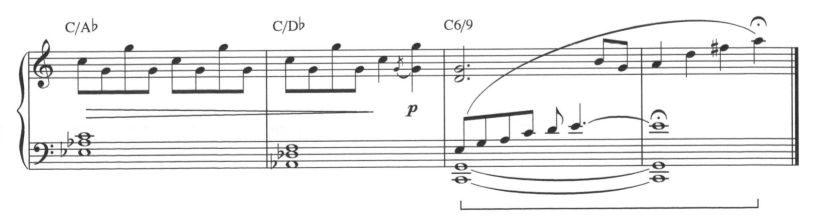

# MY SHIP
## from the Musical Production LADY IN THE DARK

Words by IRA GERSHWIN
Music by KURT WEILL

**Easy Swing**

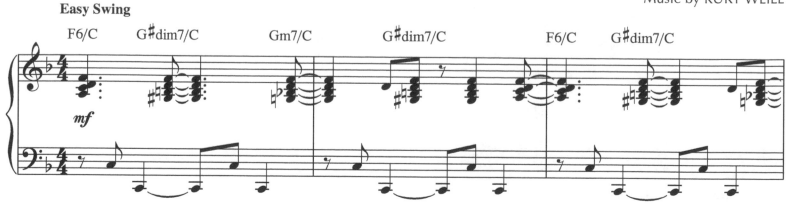

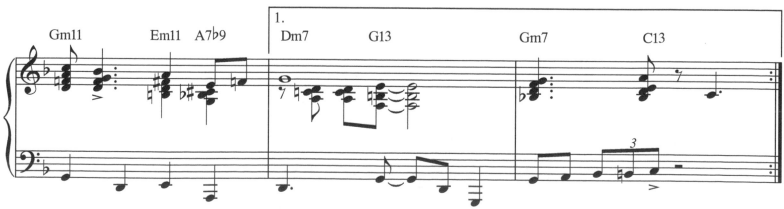

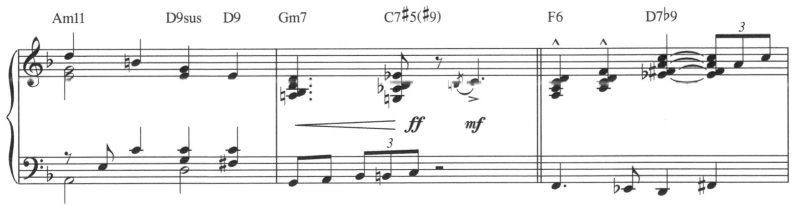

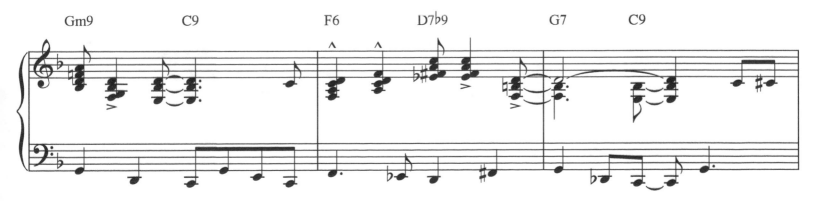

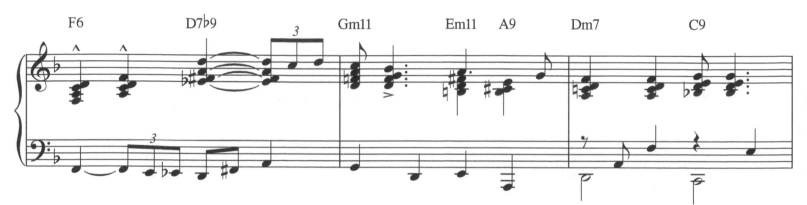

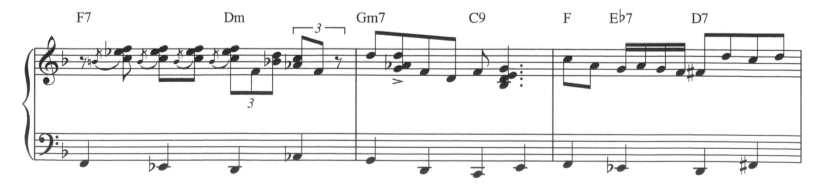

**D.S. al Coda**

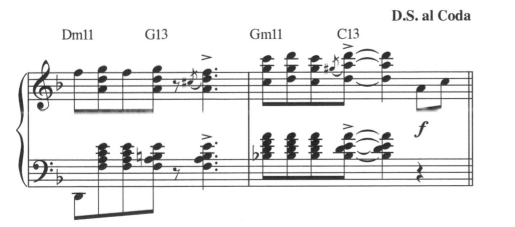

**CODA**

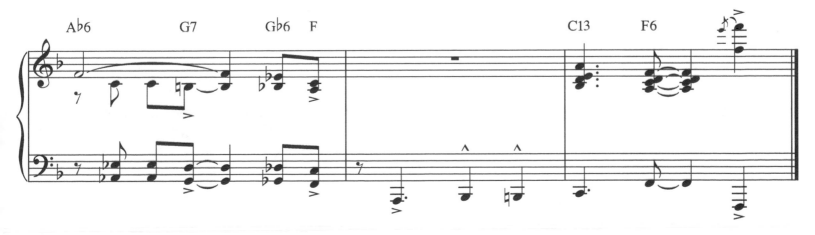

# PRELUDE TO A KISS

Words by IRVING GORDON and IRVING MILLS
Music by DUKE ELLINGTON

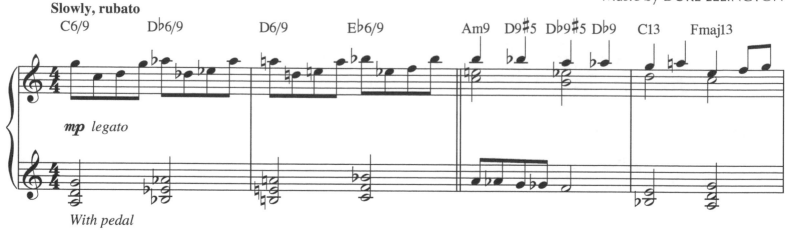

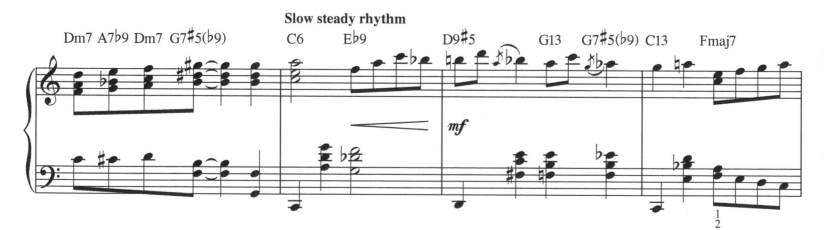

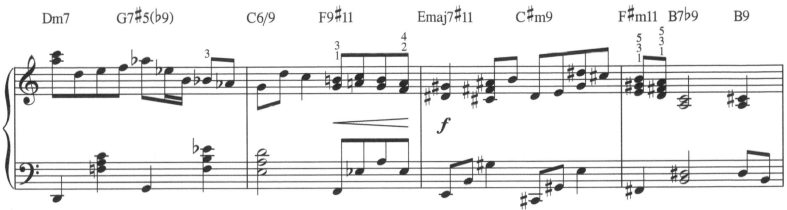

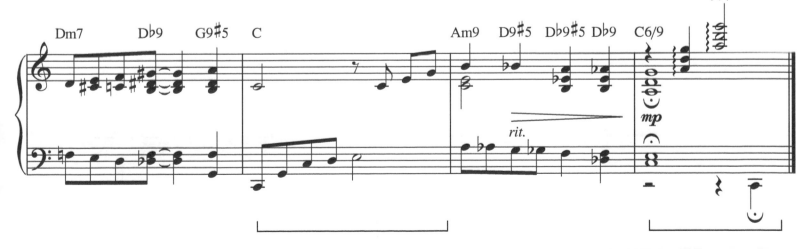

# TAKING A CHANCE ON LOVE

Words by JOHN LA TOUCHE and TED FETTER
Music by VERNON DUKE

**Whimsically**

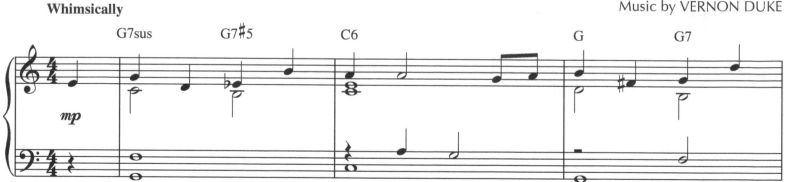

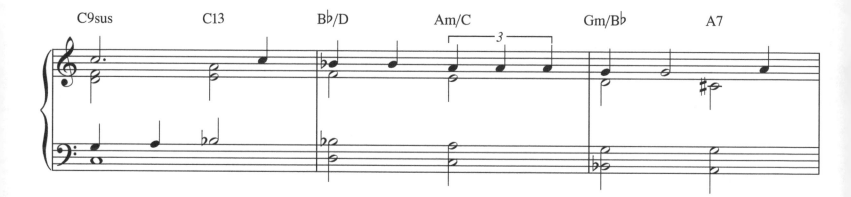

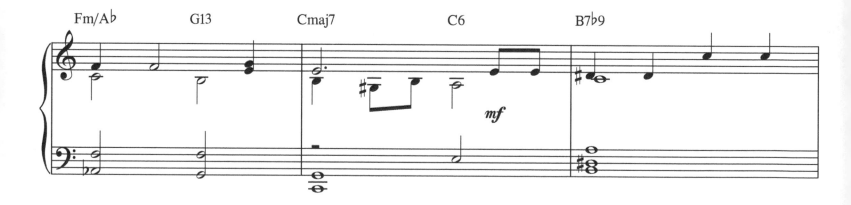

**Medium Swing**

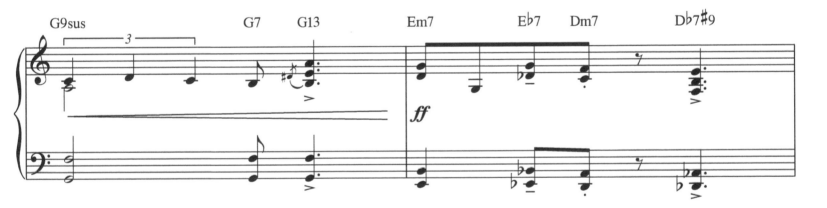

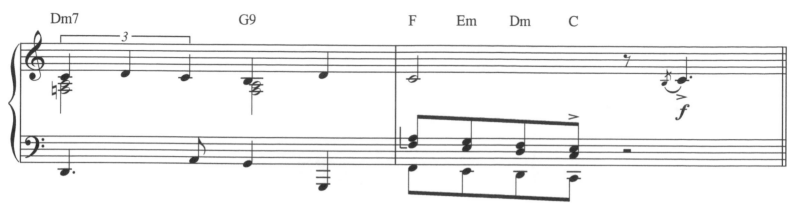

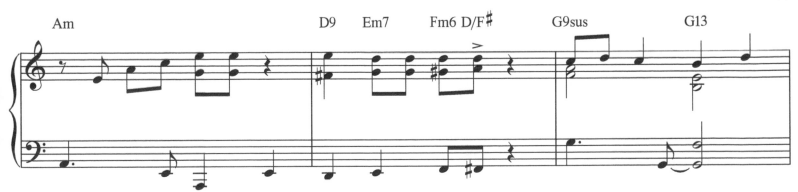

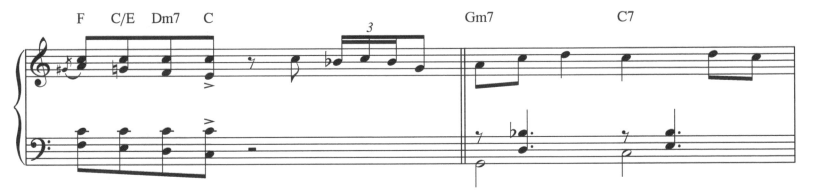

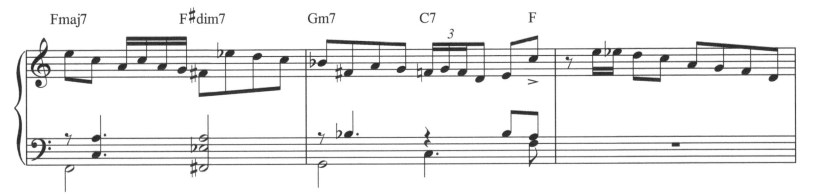

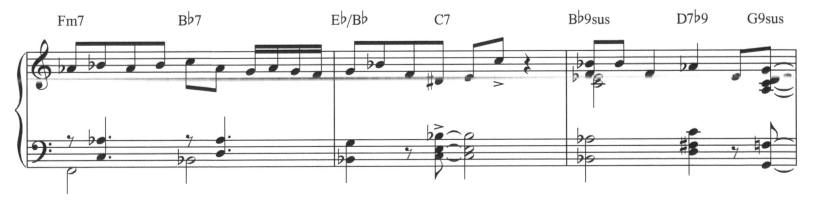

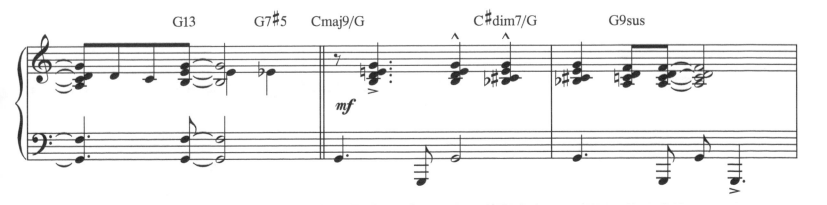

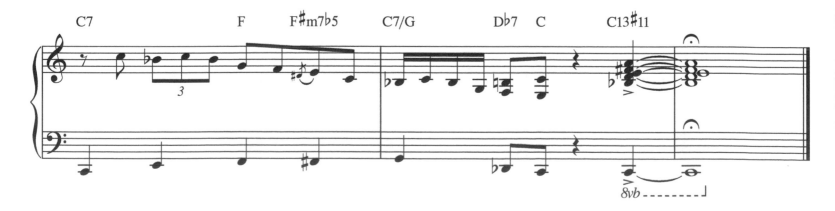

# TIME AFTER TIME

Words by SAMMY CAHN
Music by JULE STYNE

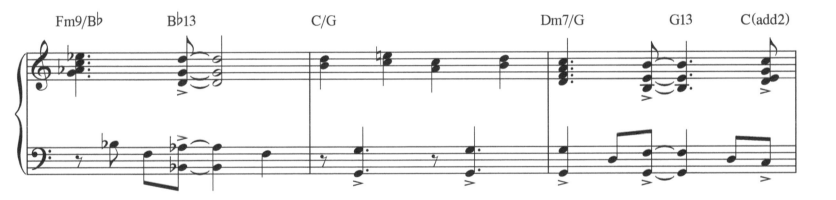

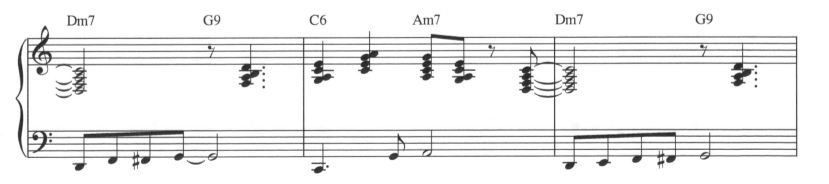

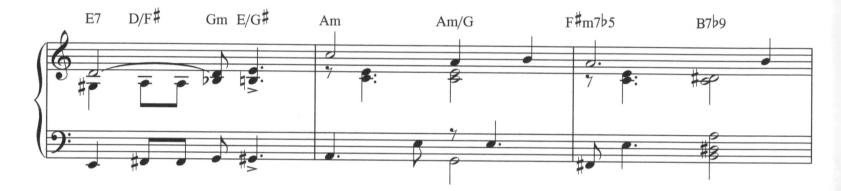

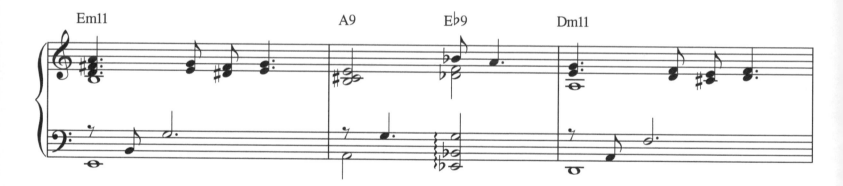

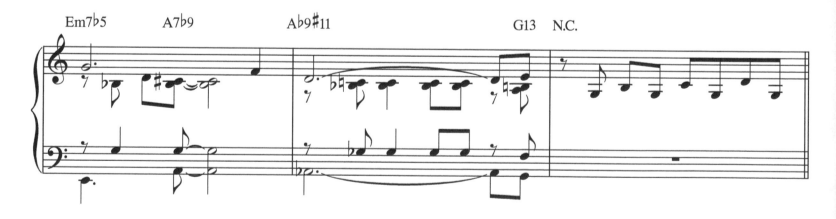

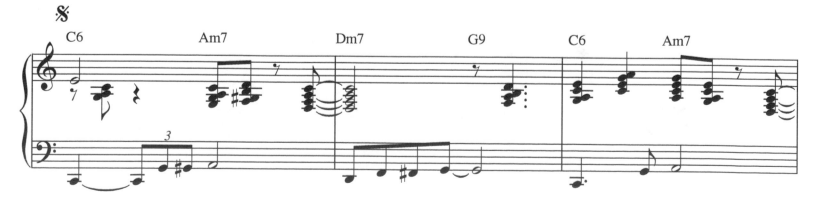

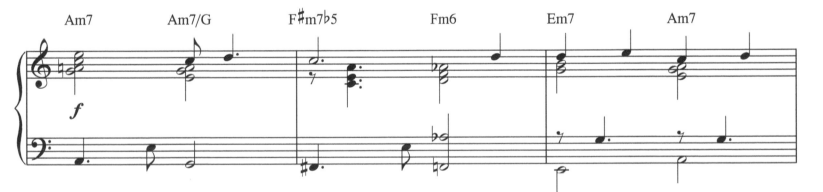

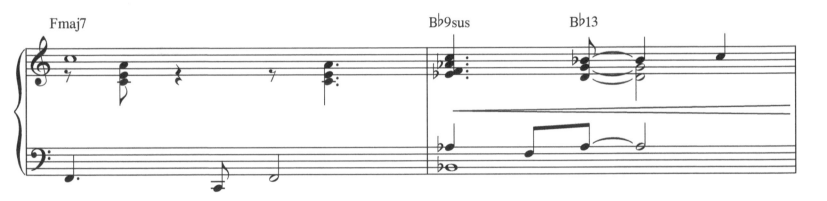

**To Coda**

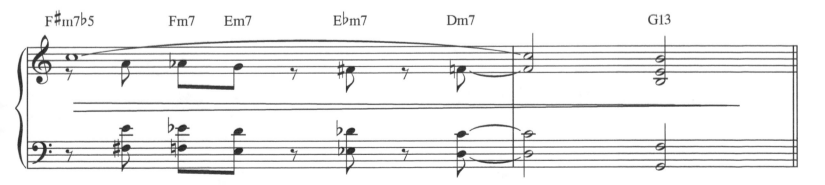

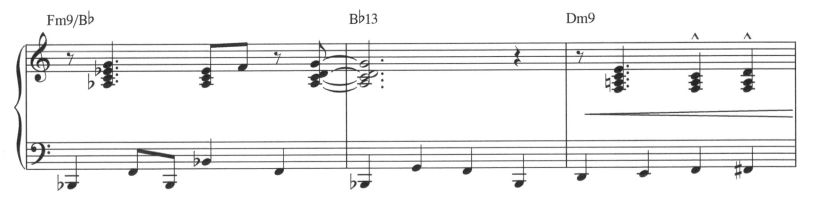

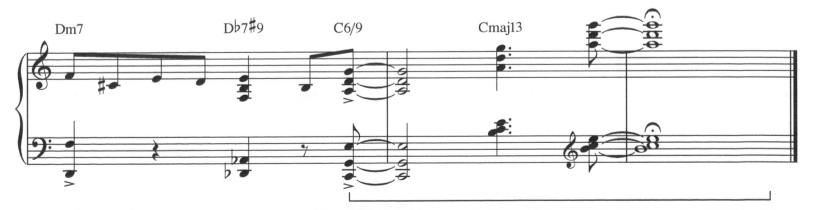

# TENDERLY
## from TORCH SONG

Lyric by JACK LAWRENCE
Music by WALTER GROSS

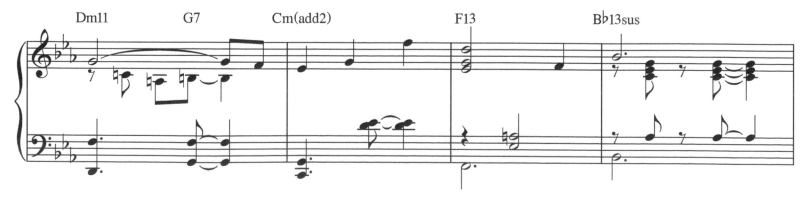

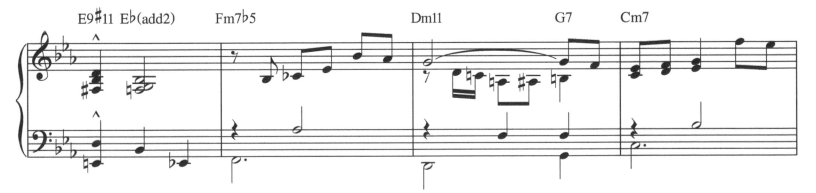

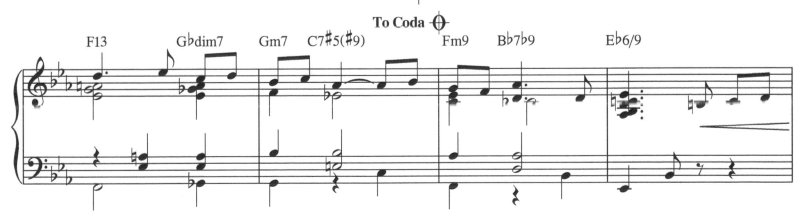

*Solo based on one by Bill Evans

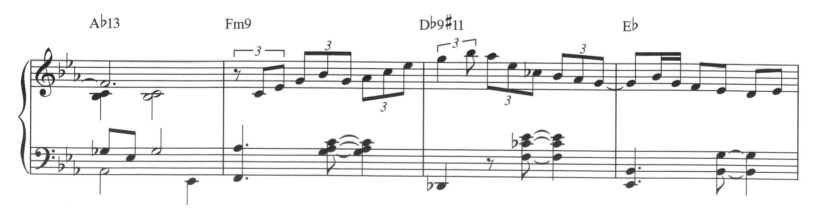

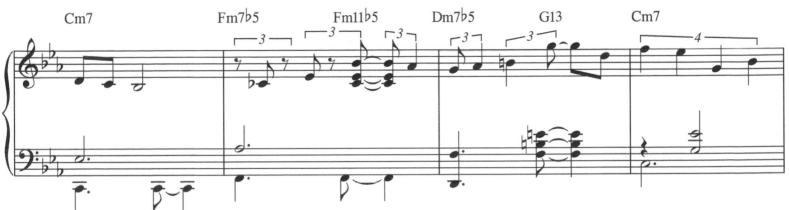

# THANKS FOR THE MEMORY

from the Paramount Picture BIG BROADCAST OF 1938

Words and Music by LEO ROBIN
and RALPH RAINGER

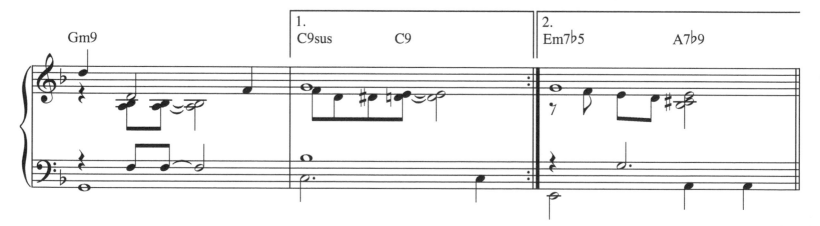

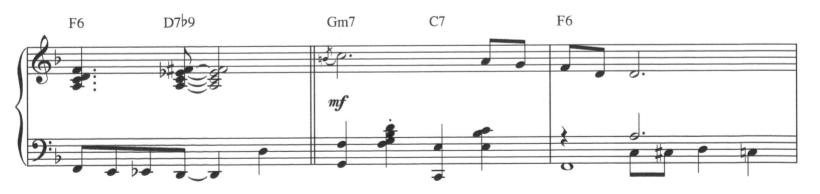

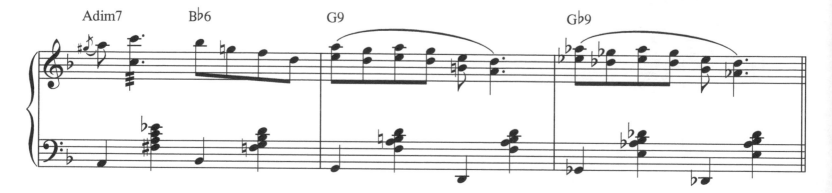

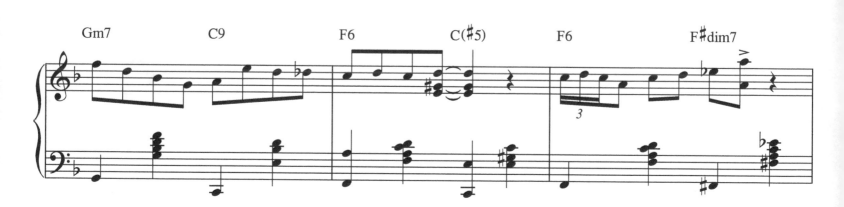

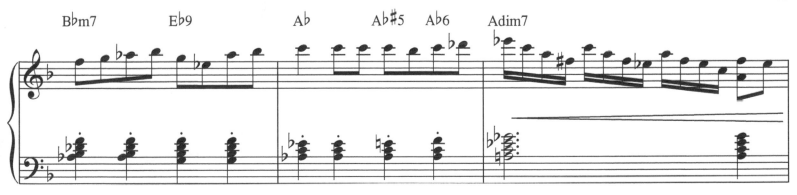

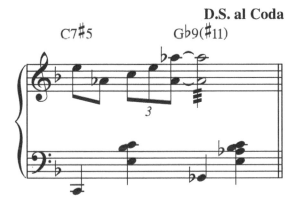

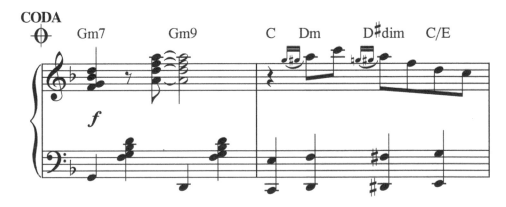

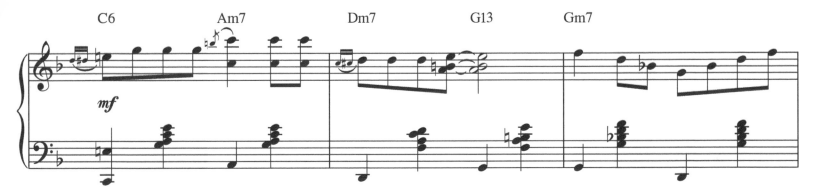

# THESE FOOLISH THINGS
## (Remind Me of You)

Words by HOLT MARVELL
Music by JACK STRACHEY

**Relaxed Swing**

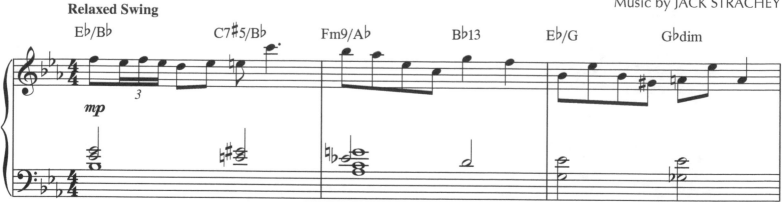

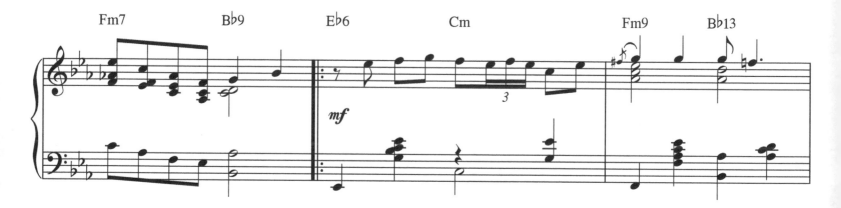

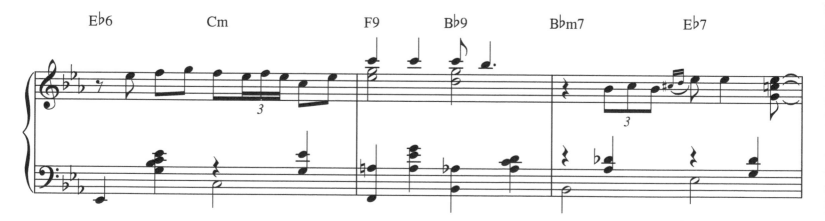

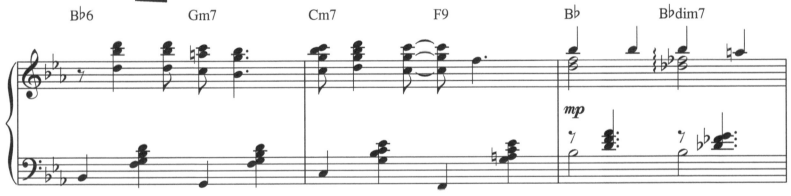

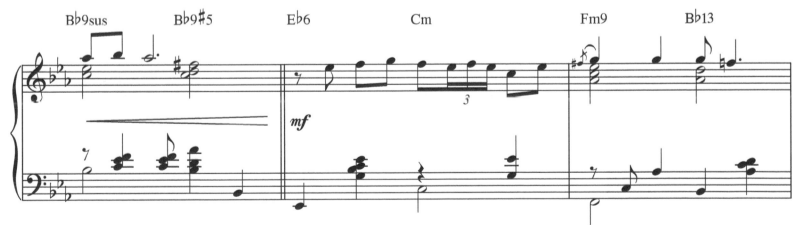

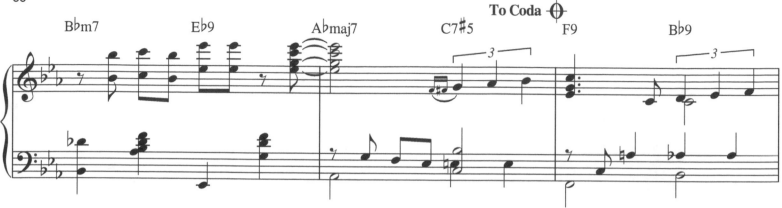

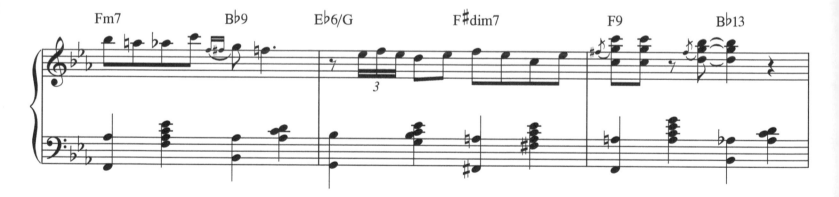

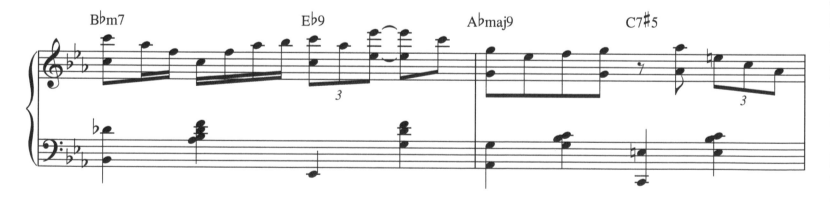

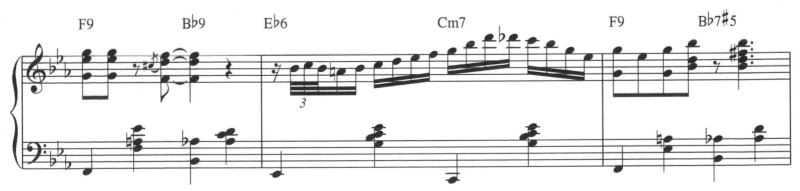

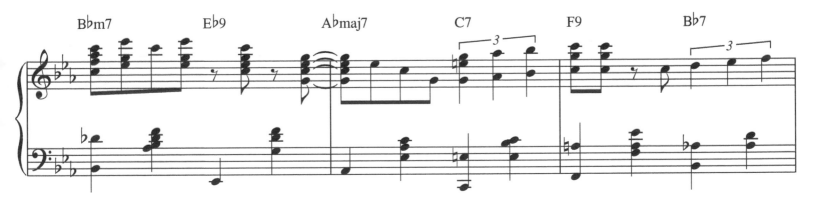

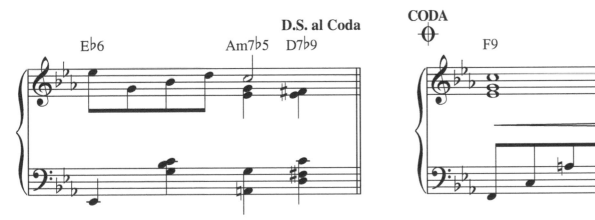

**D.S. al Coda**

**CODA**

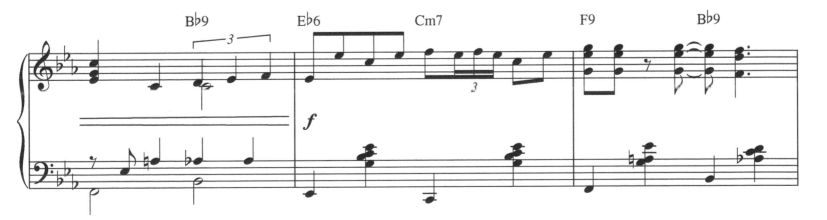

# YOU GO TO MY HEAD

Words by HAVEN GILLESPIE
Music by J. FRED COOTS

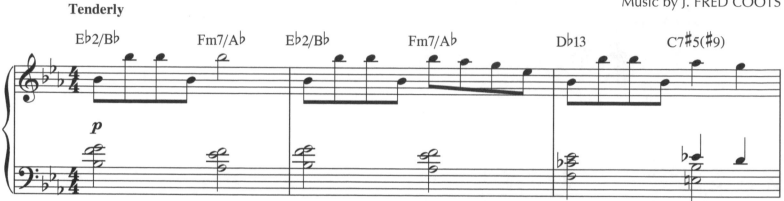

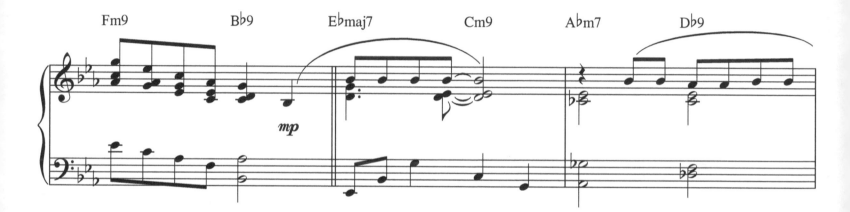

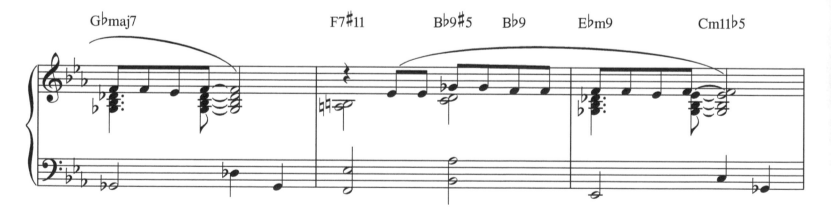

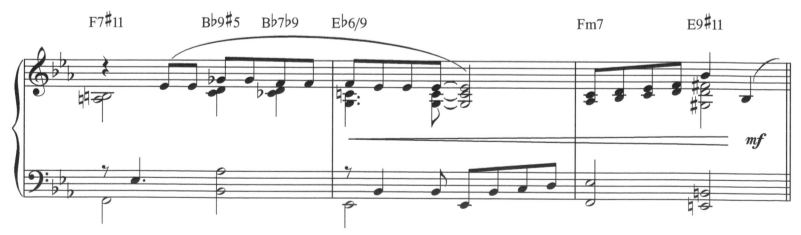

**Lilting Swing**

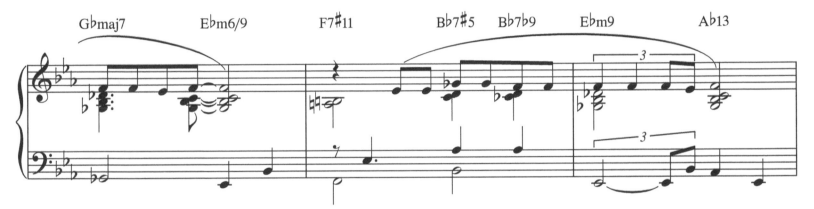

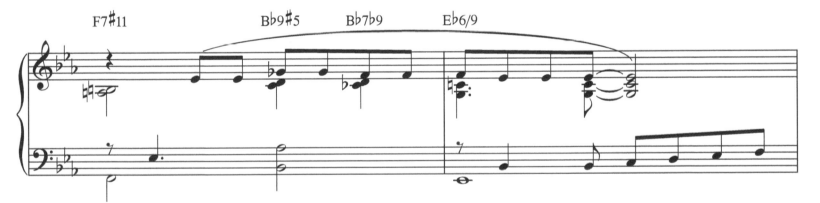

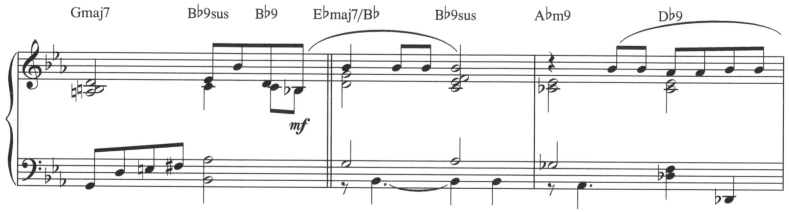

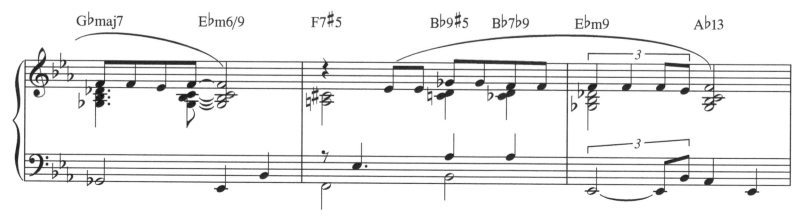

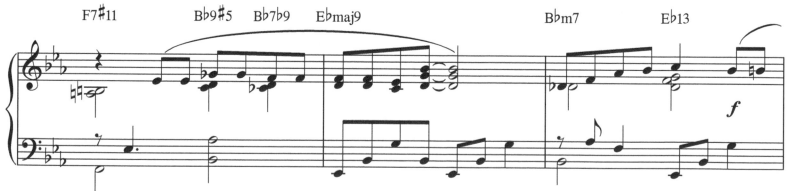

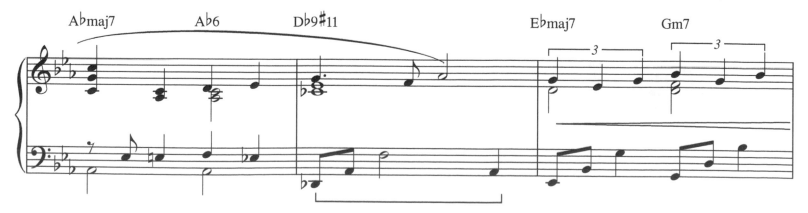

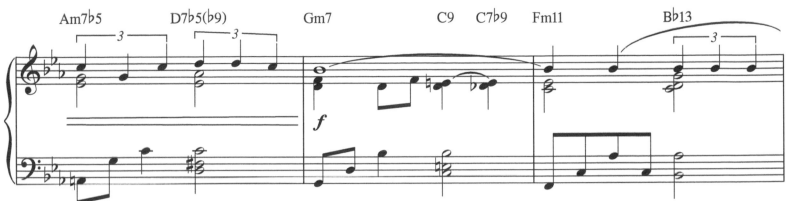

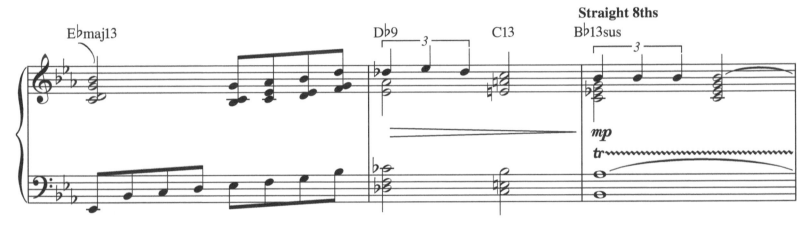

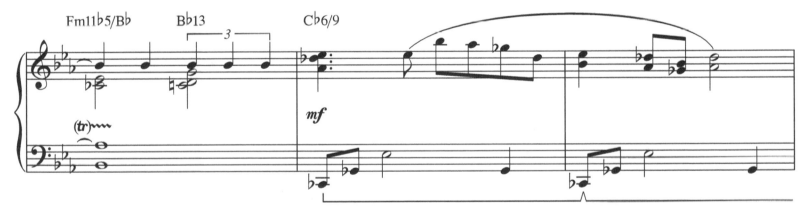

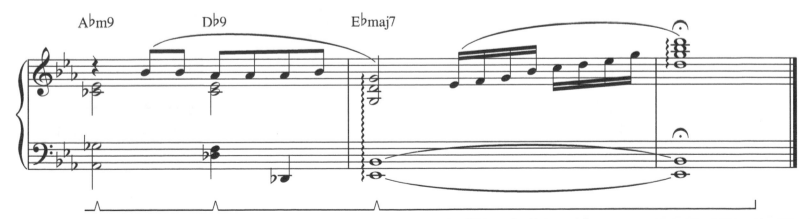

# YOU ARE TOO BEAUTIFUL

from HALLELUJAH, I'M A BUM

Words by LORENZ HART
Music by RICHARD RODGERS

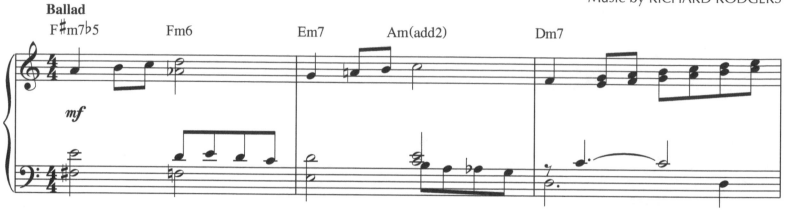

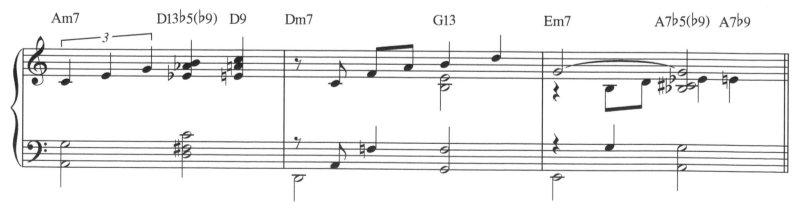

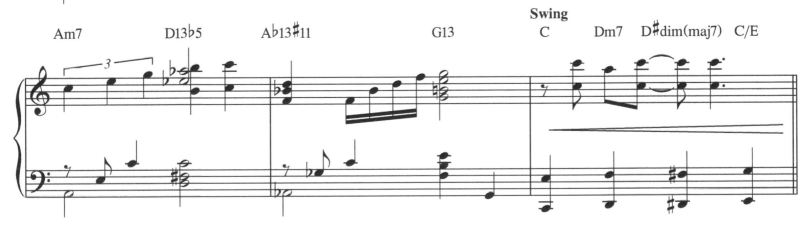

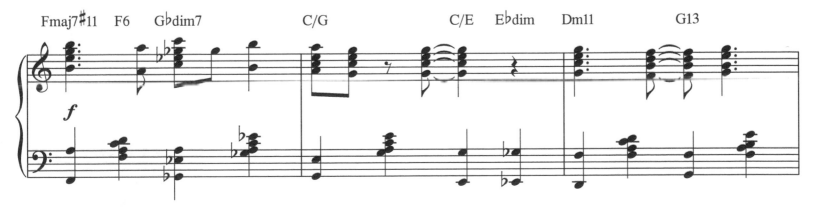

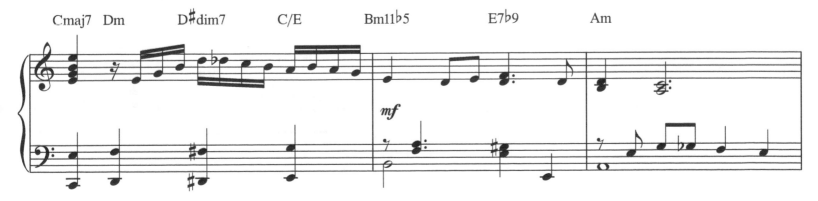

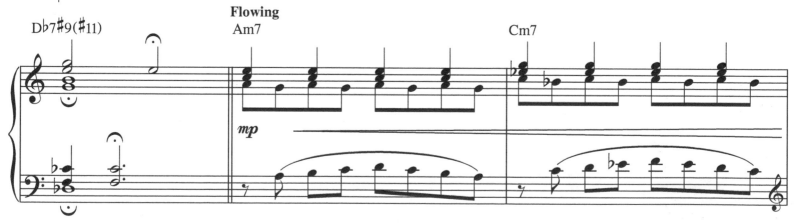

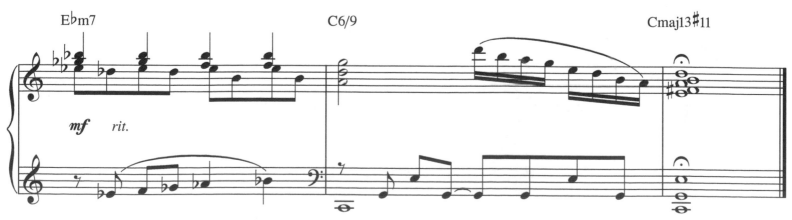